# NICCOLÒ MACHIAVELLI

**VIBS**

Volume 226

Robert Ginsberg
**Founding Editor**

Leonidas Donskis
**Executive Editor**

**Associate Editors**

| | |
|---|---|
| G. John M. Abbarno | Steven V. Hicks |
| George Allan | Richard T. Hull |
| Gerhold K. Becker | Michael Krausz |
| Raymond Angelo Belliotti | Olli Loukola |
| Kenneth A. Bryson | Mark Letteri |
| C. Stephen Byrum | Vincent L. Luizzi |
| Robert A. Delfino | Adrianne McEvoy |
| Rem B. Edwards | J.D. Mininger |
| Malcolm D. Evans | Peter A. Redpath |
| Roland Faber | Arleen L. F. Salles |
| Andrew Fitz-Gibbon | John R. Shook |
| Francesc Forn i Argimon | Eddy Souffrant |
| Daniel B. Gallagher | Tuija Takala |
| William C. Gay | Emil Višňovský |
| Dane R. Gordon | Anne Waters |
| J. Everet Green | James R. Watson |
| Heta Aleksandra Gylling | John R. Welch |
| Matti Häyry | Thomas Woods |
| Brian G. Henning | |

a volume in
**Philosophy, Literature, and Politics**
**PLP**
Leonidas Donskis and J.D. Mininger, Editors

# NICCOLÒ MACHIAVELLI
## History, Power, and Virtue

Edited by
Leonidas Donskis

Amsterdam - New York, NY 2011

Cover image. Santi di Tito: Portrait of Machiavelli. Palazzo Vechio, Florence, Italy.
(Used with permission of the Florentine Civic Museums)

Cover Design: Studio Pollmann

The paper on which this book is printed meets the requirements of "ISO 9706:1994, Information and documentation - Paper for documents - Requirements for permanence".

ISBN: 978-90-420-3277-4
E-Book ISBN: 978-90-420-3278-1
© Editions Rodopi B.V., Amsterdam - New York, NY 2011
Printed in the Netherlands

The editor of this volume owes a great debt of gratitude to
Dr. Eugenijus Gentvilas and the foundation,
VŠĮ "Atvira visuomenė ir jos draugai,"
for ideas and support that made this book possible

# CONTENTS

Editor's Foreword ... ix

## Part One
## Machiavelli's Keywords: The New Political and Moral Vocabulary

ONE: Against All the Odds: Machiavelli on Fortune in Politics
TIMO AIRAKSINEN ... 3

TWO: Border-Value Morality and Semantical Coherence in Machiavelli's *Prince*
HUBERT SCHLEICHERT ... 15

THREE: Niccolò Machiavelli on Power
MANFRED J. HOLLER ... 27

FOUR: The Modern Who Believed that He Was the Ancient: Niccolò Machiavelli in European Thought and Political Imagination
LEONIDAS DONSKIS ... 49

FIVE: Machiavelli and the Theory of Exemplary Constitutions
CĂTĂLIN AVRAMESCU ... 67

## Part Two
## Machiavelli and Core Issues in Modern Political Philosophy

SIX: Virtue in Hobbes: Seen from Machiavellian Point of View
JUHANA LEMETTI ... 79

SEVEN: Rethinking Machiavelli: Republicanism and Tolerance
OLLI LOUKOLA ... 91

Contributors ... 109

Index ... 111

Santi di Tito, *Portrait of Niccolò Machiavelli*

# EDITOR'S FOREWORD

This book is the outcome of a series of international seminars on Niccolò Machiavelli and early modern European political philosophy held at Vytautas Magnus University School of Political Science and Diplomacy in Kaunas, Lithuania. The group of scholars, who contributed their articles to this volume, started acting as an academic network made up by colleagues from Finland, Germany, Romania, Estonia, and Lithuania.

This collections of articles is an attempt to rethink Machiavelli, one of the most challenging and provocative political thinkers in the history of European ideas and political thought. In 2013, we will mark five hundred years since Machiavelli wrote his puzzling letter to Lorenzo de' Medici, *Il Principe* (*The Prince*, written in 1513, and published in 1532). We are able to study the logic and the dynamics of European political thought on the grounds of its hostile reactions or highly positive attitudes to the body of ideas, concepts, insights, metaphors, and other figures of speech worked out and put together by Machiavelli in *The Prince*. Although nearly every scholar keeps repeating that *Discourses on Livy* far surpasses *The Prince* in terms of scholarly weight, erudition, learning, and intellectual value, *The Prince* does remain one of the landmark documents of Renaissance political thought.

However, this book is part of an academic endeavor to embrace the hidden and complex aspects of Niccolò Machiavelli's life and work. It reflects the editor's sincere wish to contribute to the field of study, which may well be described as the Machiavelli studies. Therefore, my heartfelt thanks are due to all contributors of the book.

For lending their skills to provide the layout of the book, I thank Linas Vaškevičius and Saulius Bajorinas. For permission to reprint the significantly changed articles of Timo Airaksinen and Manfred J. Holler, I owe a debt of gratitude, respectively, to ACCEDO Verlag and Frankfurt School Verlag.

Last but not least, I wish to thank my colleagues and friends Eric van Broekhuizen and J. D. Mininger for their support and understanding, which resulted in this volume that initiates the new book sub-series for the VIBS-Value Inquiry Book Series with Rodopi – Philosophy, Literature, and Politics.

L. D.<br>
Brussels, Belgium<br>
10 September 2010

Part One

# MACHIAVELLI'S KEYWORDS: THE NEW POLITICAL AND MORAL VOCABULARY

One

# AGAINST ALL THE ODDS: MACHIAVELLI ON FORTUNE IN POLITICS*

Timo Airaksinen

**Abstract**

Machiavelli explains the success of princes by referring to their *virtú*, or prowess which overcomes the vagaries of fortune. I pay attention to the meaning of *virtú*, which some commentators claim to be a clear and understandable term while others deny this. If *virtú* is defined in terms of fortune, we have reasons to be skeptical. The problem is that fortune is a concept of many meanings in *The Prince*. Some of these are mythological, such as the goddess Fortune and fortune as a woman. Machiavelli seems to use the concept of fortune in four different ways: resource, fate or destiny, chance, and uncertainty. I will provide evidence for this thesis as I analyze these ideas and try to relate them to each other. *The Prince* is a conceptually loose treatise.

## 1. The Political Animal

Niccolò Machiavelli's famous political vision is too metaphorical, rhetorical, and narrative to qualify as philosophy. Alternatively, it is a grand political theory which leads us beyond all the small scale analytical understanding to the world of lofty metaphysics of effective action, politics, and social power. It paints a picture of the political realm as a battlefield where some exceptional individuals may survive if they play their cards right. Otherwise, they perish. But they do not perish alone. With them goes, into oblivion, their principalities or city states. Actually, in this grand perspective, it may not make much sense to draw a distinction between *The Prince* and his city-state. Machiavelli speaks as if he would like to maintain this distinction, as if the man, *The Prince*, and his realm would be two different things. But all this is a rhetorical illusion created with a skillful hand and designed to deceive the reader. Actually, the man and his realm are not two separate entities. They belong together,

---

* A significantly modified version of this paper was published under the tittle "Fortune is a Woman: Machiavelli on Luck and Virtue," in *Essays in Honor of Hannu Nurmi, Homo Oeconomicus* 26 (2009), pp. 551–568, Manfred J. Holler and Mika Widgren (eds). Permission to reprint is granted by ACCEDO Verlag.

they live together, and they die together. Why would someone risk everything to possess a city-state and guarantee its safety in that universal war that was Renaissance Italy? Why would the successful men be such extraordinary individuals? Why should they battle against all the odds in a monomaniac manner dedicating their lives to only one noble cause? They have no ethics, no religion, no happiness, and no life to live, except when they struggle to keep that most elusive of all possessions (power) to themselves. However, one might even argue that they have no power. If they had power, they could relax and see themselves as individual persons free of their constrictive roles as princes and rulers. But they have no power. They struggle all the time to stay alive alone in a world that entitles them to minimal value and guarantees them nothing. They are as weak and powerless as their states which survive for a while and then collapse. A new prince comes and tries his hand at power. History runs its course and these brave men along with it. They are their own city-states. Their destinies are tied together in a way in which we can only understand through a historical narrative.

A person may not have much power against the ruthless fate and forces of time and history.[1] Yet there is hope as the ancient Roman World and its enduring success shows.[2] It is not impossible to survive and even flourish. But Machiavelli's own Italy is different. Its princes battle endlessly and try their personal luck against foreign barbarian and local competitors, unable to expect much success. They must be swift, ruthless, violent, and clever.[3] As they have no power, they need to act. Power allows you to stop, relax, and look around. Machiavelli's prince can never relax. He moves, plans, and acts all the time. He is a creature of strategy and cunning whose only interest is survival. Such a meager goal is the final cause of politics and, at the same time, the reason why politics has always been despised by those who have power, religious, intellectual, or even traditional political power.

Of course Machiavelli compares his princes to different types of animals. They are animals in their relentless urge to live and survive in changing circumstance in the middle of other animals. Their wisdom is of the animal kind which is more than understandable. Compare these two quotations. First, a Roman emperor:

> So whoever carefully studies what this man [Severus] did will find that he had the qualities of ferocious lion and a very cunning fox, and that he was feared and respected by everyone, yet not hated by the troops… Severus, an upstart, proved himself able to maintain such great power.

Next, Machiavelli's own Italy is different:

> Those who are capable are not obeyed. Everyone imagines he is competent, and hitherto no one has had the competence to dominate the others by means of his prowess and good fortune. As a result of this, over so long a

time, in so many wars during the past twenty years, when there has been an all-Italian army, it has always given a bad account of itself...[4]

In the glorious Roman past some men had prowess, or *virtú*, and good luck, or *Fortune*. They had *virtú* and Madam *Fortune* on their side. They were animals, and very strange animals they were. They were like centaurs and chimaeras that were put together from sets of mutually incompatible parts. Severus is, at the same time, a lion and a fox exhibiting qualities which any storyteller would reserve for two different and separate creatures. In order to succeed you need to be a very improbable animal which is no longer possible in Machiavelli's Italy. Now men are men and not fictional creatures of imagination. They imagine they are competent, but when they act it is evident that they have no *virtú* and not much luck. They struggle and lose, powerless, but for ever trying to turn the tables. All they do is give a bad account of themselves. Power was available to Severus a long time ago, but for moderns it is a mere illusion based on one's imagination. Men are no longer animals. They know too much, they imagine too much, they are under too many constraints, and they fail because of all this. They are no longer mythical creatures of the past; the unfamiliar combinations of foxes and lions. Yet they should do something to survive together with their principalities. They are their states, and when they fail and collapse everything is lost. Foreign barbarians will come and dominate. The stakes are high so the measures against bad fortune must always be forceful and extreme. The battle reaches cosmic proportions simply because it is a symbolic equivalent of the end of the world, a cosmic catastrophe which rages till the paradise comes back to earth. It is a battle for the new Rome, if not Jerusalem. Machiavelli's deepest hopes are messianic. The second coming may be near:

> I asked myself whether in present-day Italy the times were propitious to honor a new prince, and whether the circumstances existed here which would make it possible for a prudent and capable man to introduce a new order, bringing honour to himself and prosperity to all and every Italian... I cannot imagine there ever was a time more suitable than the present.[5]

## 2. The Meaning of *Virtú*

Some funny things have been said about Machiavelli's political mythology and his political animals. Quentin Skinner and George Bull (the translator of the Penguin edition of *The Prince*) directly contradict each other about the definition of *virtú*. Skinner writes as follows:

> It is often complained that Machiavelli fails to provide any definition of *virtú*, and even that (as Whitfield puts it) he is "innocent of any systematic use of the word." But it will now be evident that he uses the term with

complete consistency. Following his classical and humanist authorities, he treats it as that quality which enables a prince to withstand the blows of Fortune, to attract the goddess's favour, and to rise in consequence to the heights of princely fame, winning honour and glory for himself and security for his government.[6]

Bull contradicts Skinner:

> A great deal has been written about the Renaissance concept of *virtú*, but Machiavelli, like his contemporaries, seems to have used it freely and loosely, nearly always in antithesis to *Fortune*, sometimes with the sense of willpower, sometimes efficiency, sometimes even with the sense of virtue.[7]

As Skinner recognizes, this controversy is a real one; yet it is not easy to see why Skinner says that *virtú* has a clear and consistent meaning if its definition rests on an account of the mythical female goddess, Fortune. In fact, Skinner refers to Fortune too, and in that respect, Skinner and Bull agree. I would think that any definition of a term which logically entails indefinable terms is not acceptable as completely clear and consistent. When we try to understand *virtú,* we are also talking about *Fortune*, and if we do not understand *Fortune*, we do not understand *virtú*. Can we say with a clear conscience that we know what *Fortune* means in Machiavelli's texts? Bull is right when he contrasts *virtú* to *Fortune*, and Skinner agrees. But what does *Fortune* mean? Once we have answered this question we begin to understand what *virtú* means. Bull translates it as prowess, which is a good choice. But when we realize that the princely prowess means one's capability and success against bad luck, we are lost. If we said that prowess means one's ability to defeat one's enemies and reach one's goals over a wide range of political circumstances, the case would be much clearer. However, *Fortune* must be mentioned simply because Machiavelli does so in *The Prince*. As I said above, this is a mythological book. It is not philosophy. It is not a guidebook for princely pretenders. It is a cosmic allegory of power lost and regained and of the lost paradise.

My own view is that the meaning of *Fortune* can be understood by looking at different context where Machiavelli uses the term; yet no clear-cut meaning emerges from this exercise. It is true that Machiavelli uses *Fortune* in many different ways, and thus the meaning of *virtú* will remain equally open. In a rhetorical and ultimately poetical work, this does not create any problems. If *The Prince* were a political manual and a guidebook the situation would be much worse. If you do not understand what its key terms mean, you cannot follow its advice.

## 3. *Fortune*, Its Use and Meanings

Machiavelli uses the concept of *Fortune* in many different ways in *The Prince*. The following four main meanings can be identified: resource, fate or destiny, chance, and uncertainty. I will try to offer evidence for this classification below. I will explain all this as systematically as possible. I also discuss each meaning from the point of view of its mythological and poetic import. Some of the contexts and usages are fully mytho-poetic, which casts a shadow over Skinner's claims about the definition of *virtú*, or prowess. We will see that only the second and perhaps the third meaning are directly relevant to the definition of *virtú*, if *virtú* is defined in antithesis to *Fortune*, as Bull puts it. The first meaning does not help us define *virtú* at all, and the last one is semantically relevant only indirectly. The first meaning of *Fortune*, a resource, is simply an alternative to *virtú*, as amazing as it may sound.

### 3. 1. Fortune as a Resource

"Fortune" means in the English language (good) luck or a large amount of money and property. Perhaps, this linguistic ambiguity is not merely coincidental. Fortune can be a resource just like property, at least in fiction and myth. Prezzolini writes as follows:

> One thing is, however, certain. For Machiavelli Fortune never means what it did for Dante (...), that is the minister of God, guided by Him, the dispenser of earthly goods which men, because of their blindness, do not see as a rational force. In other words, Machiavelli's Fortune does not correspond to a divine and rational design.[8]

De Grazia seems to say the same about this mysterious and "perverse being": "It is the most serious threat to political action," that is, it certainly is not a hidden rational plan. Then he says: "Dominions are acquired, among other ways, 'by fortune or by virtue'."[9] Notice how clumsily these two sentences fit together: if one can acquire a dominion by means of fortune, it cannot always be a threat to one's successful political action. This shows how difficult it is to paint the picture of Fortune and sketch her role in political affairs.

Let us try to find evidence for the resource view of (good) fortune. I already quoted Machiavelli above; in his words, "competence to dominate the others by means of his prowess and good fortune" place *virtú* and *Fortune* in parallel positions as means and resources to be used in order to be successful in battle and politics.[10] One can put fortune to use just like one uses one's specious *virtú*. This may sound strange, but I am sure this is one of the normal and traditional uses of "fortune" and "luck." It is a mythological way of thinking which is preserved in our day, although one would well be advised not to use it in any discursive or theoretical manner in a serious context. Somehow, I would love to be able to be lucky in the sense that I could *use* my good luck to be successful. Of course, I know this is not the case, but I still dream about it. I am a lucky person, which is to say that I have that rare resource at my disposal.

Machiavelli writes: "A prince wins them [dominions] either with the arms of others or his own, either by fortune or by prowess."[11] This quotation is from the opening paragraph of *The Prince*, which gives it special importance. It is fortunate to be able to benefit from the arms of others or from something which does not belong to him. In this case he is lucky, and he wins by means of his luck. This shows that it is possible to win by means of luck. This does mean, however, that one can use luck to win if one just happens to be lucky.

Machiavelli resorts here to his most powerful mythological imagery, Fortune as a woman:

> I hold strongly to this: that it is better to be impetuous than circumspect; because fortune is a woman and if she is to be submissive it is necessary to beat and coerce her. Experience shows that she is more often subdued by men who do this than by those who act coldly.[12]

It is, so to speak, possible to exploit fortune and the services of Fortune or Lady Luck. Notice that it is better to act impetuously or rush to action and take one's chances than it is to wait. This is to exploit Fortune as a resource. All this is wishful thinking, of course, or an atavistic dream, but Machiavelli's account of luck would not be complete without it. His prince may feel like a gambler who goes to the roulette table in order to make a large sum of money. He assures himself that he can use the wheel to his own advantage, and that it may even represent his only chance to get rich.

Machiavelli says that there are two ways of becoming a prince, "by prowess or by fortune." He continues: "duke Valentino, acquired his state through the good fortune of his father, and lost it when that disappeared." Later Machiavelli writes: "So whoever studies that man's [Agathocles] actions will discover little or nothing that can be attributed to fortune…"[13] Here fortune is again a resource which may disappear, and then one is in trouble. Agathocles, on the contrary, is a man who refuses to use luck; he does not need it. He is so resourceful that *Fortune*, as an additional resource, is not needed. He does not want that woman.

### 3. 2. Fortune as Fate and Destiny

The following view presented by Crick is puzzling:

> By now it should be clear that in no sense can Machiavelli be called a determinist. Indeed, he constantly praises free actions; only, he insists, actions take place in some social and historical context. Necessity narrows the range of alternatives, but choices have to be made. Further, it is possible by reason applied to experience to make meaningful generalizations (…)

about how likely certain types of action are to succeed in certain types of circumstance (but even then, there is always *Fortune*).[14]

Fortune is now something like a side constraint and a deterministically understood fate or destiny, the blind force of necessity, and it becomes the main obstacle. Crick first rejects this view which is understandable, but then he goes all the way to unfounded voluntarism. Of course, it is true that a prince must make choices, and it is equally true that the success of these choices is always dependent on luck. He can plan his action, this is trivially true, and he may succeed in spite of bad luck, this is also true. But it is still difficult to see how "necessity narrows the range of alternatives."[15] The only possible interpretation which I can see here is to say that some alternatives are too dangerous to try. Some political and military moves, given their social and historical context, are so risky that they should not be attempted. Whatever the action is, it may be successful, but in some cases the agent judges the odds to be negligible. He must not act, although he might get lucky and succeed. Anything can happen, but only a fool bets on it.

Fortune means here fate and blind destiny or pure negativity which fails you and makes all your plans void.[16] In this sense, Fortune gets a pseudo-deterministic interpretation, although such a formulation may be dangerously misleading. Nevertheless, it has its important message as well. When luck is understood as pure negativity it is destiny which can be understood – almost – as a deterministic force. I fight a losing battle against a superior enemy. This case can be interpreted in two ways: it is my bad luck that I find myself in such a desperate situation, and it is my destiny to lose everything. I can do nothing to change the situation, therefore I am doomed. In such a case, luck and destiny overlap, or they can be identified. My bad luck turns out to be my destiny. Machiavelli plays with these ideas in many places throughout *The Prince*.

Machiavelli writes: "I believe that it is probably true that fortune is the arbiter of half of the things we do, leaving the other half or so controlled by ourselves. I compare fortune to one of those violent rivers…there is no possibility of resistance."[17] Along with this sober position, the following also makes sense: "The only sound, sure, and enduring methods of defense are those based on your own actions and prowess."[18] If you can control only approximately half of the success relevant factors, what else can you do but rely on your own capabilities? After acting, you hope for success since you can do nothing else. No man is strong enough to control his own future. It all depends on your fate as if it were written on the stars. Or if you do not want to think in this way, you just admit that there is a limit to what you can do and achieve.

It is obvious that this account of fortune is inconsistent with the one we called luck as a resource. Fifty percent of all situational determinants are beyond my control, thus it does not make any sense to say that I may rely on my luck or use it for my benefit. The cruel irony of the following story illustrates my case perfectly:

And he himself said to me, the day Julius II was elected, that he had thought of everything that could happen when his father died, and found a remedy for everything, except that he never thought that when he did so he himself would be at the point of death.[19]

Notice also the following point: "...unless it commands its own arms no principality is secure; rather, it is dependent on fortune, since there is no valour and no loyalty to defend it when adversity comes."[20] Such a principality is at the mercy on totally unknown forces; nothing can be done.

### 3. 3. Fortune as Chance

Here we approach luck and fortune as something which resembles our own contemporary notions. Machiavelli can be seen as a supporter of an idea of chance in a *synchronic* context in the following sense. Think of the game of Russian Roulette. The idea is simple. There are, say, six players, you take a six shooter revolver, you load it with one live cartridge, and finally you turn the drum randomly. Now, the game begins. The first player aims the barrel of the revolver at his temple and pulls the trigger. He dies or he does not die. The drum is turned again into a random position. Then the next player pulls the trigger; and so they continue until only one player survives. He is the winner who reaps the benefits, whatever they happen to be. The rules of the game are perfectly fair because every player has the same chance of staying alive, 1/6 to be exact. In this game one cannot exploit *Fortune* in any way. One is at the mercy of Lady Luck in the most obvious way, as long as the revolver circulates among the players. The winner may call himself lucky but only after the game. We often talk about good and bad luck in hindsight when we mean chance.

Is such a synchronic notion of fortune really different from the idea of negativity of luck discussed above? It is different, at least, in the sense that we can now estimate probabilities and calculate the chances. Machiavelli said that fifty percent of our successes depend on us, the rest does not. It does not matter how we call this fifty percent – it is there, and that is all we can say about it. Something unexpected is prone to happen in whatever we do and /or wherever we are. A bullet may hit your armor and bounce off, or it may hit your unprotected parts. If it hurts you, you may still survive, or perhaps you may die. These are general possibilities which cannot be calculated, estimated, or predicted in any way. Everything is possible. Chance is different. In the game of Russian Roulette we know exactly what the a priori chances are. We just cannot utilize this knowledge in any way. Knowledge is not always power. But, on the other hand, the pure negativity of fortune also means that knowledge may be an ever impossible option. In this sense, it is clear that there is a difference between the negativity of luck and synchronic chance. We know how to handle chance and estimate its value, and sometimes we may even utilize this knowledge. If two groups of Russian roulette players invite me to play with them, I may choose the group with the smaller number of players if the rewards are equal. In this case, knowledge is power. But the present notion of synchronic chance applies only to the playing of the game itself; then I am at the mercy of *Fortune*. Machiavelli knows such cases well:

> Then, no government should ever imagine that it can always adopt a safe course; rather, it should regard all possible course of action as risky. This is the way things are: whenever one tries to escape one danger one runs into another. Prudence consists in being able to assess the nature of a particular threat and accepting the lesser evil.[21]

One is able to calculate the synchronic chances and their associated risks, and one must do so. It is not enough to know that fifty percent is beyond one's control, one must be able to do better calculations. Action alternatives must be compared in some rational manner. They are all presented as here-and-now scenarios, and then they are compared, and the best alternative is chosen. This presupposes that some calculations of chance can be made. If one very harmful scenario is also extremely unlikely to happen, then it can be discarded. *The Prince* must be able to calculate the relevant chances, and then he can plan ahead. After he has made his best possible plan, he can act according to it, and then, once again, he needs good luck. Even the best plan can fail because of some new and unpredictable events and circumstances. Bad weather or an outbreak of venereal disease among his troops my turn out to be catastrophic. That is a truely bad luck.

### 3. 4. Fortune as Uncertainty

We now move from synchronic to diachronic considerations. The task is to find the best possible action strategy from several alternatives and realize it, thus, minimizing the loss or maximizing the gain. Machiavelli seems to anticipate the idea of this kind of planning and its theory (see that last quotation above). Once we know what is likely to happen, one should optimize the risk. This can be of no surprise as he wants to guide *The Prince* through danger and intrigue all the way to success, at least this is the surface message of *The Prince*. He needs to narrate some strategies of success.

But what is the difference between this fourth meaning of *Fortune* and the third as described above in the last quotation? Now we are discussing a "well regulated power to resist her [Fortune]." We discuss an engineering problem or our need for "embankments and dykes built to restrain her."[22] Even if the *Fortune* is like "violent rivers," it can be controlled. Notice, by the way, the clumsy metaphor Machiavelli uses here: a woman as a violent river. When he calls fortune a woman, Fortune, he says that a man of *virtù* needs to beat her to submission. This is his most famous allegory. The next one is less know, and it is the one which does not fit the first one, Fortune as a violent river which cannot be controlled but which needs strong borders which keeps her at bay. It is remarkable that Machiavelli's Fortune can be coerced and beaten to submission, but she is also an unstoppable force which can only be gently directed to a new path. Fortune can be stopped and she cannot be stopped. These clumsy inconsistencies indicate the manner in which Machiavelli uses the concept of fortune, and these ways are not always mutually consistent. Now we discuss the constraints, embankments and dykes, which control the ever threatening Fortune. Of course, we cannot control Fortune, so here Machiavelli exaggerates. What he actually means is that *The Prince* controls himself, so that he minimizes the threat of bad luck. The embankments and dykes are his own mental constructions which help him to stay on the right track. Machiavelli speaks as if we could engineer controls against the vagaries of luck, but he does not really believe in this idea. In his text, Machiavelli gives some sober advice to princes and asks them to make carefully calculated, balanced choices which minimize the potential losses in crisis situations and in the world When Machiavelli describes crises he means a normal state of affairs. *The Prince* must be ready.

Machiavelli writes:

> This also explains why prosperity is ephemeral; because if a man behaves with patience and circumspection and the time and circumstances are such that this method is called for, he will prosper; but if time and circumstances change he will be ruined because he does not change his policy. ...If he changed his character according to the time and circumstances, then his fortune would not change.[23]

The problems is that "those princes who are utterly dependent on fortune come to grief when their fortune changes."[24] What is Machiavelli saying here? One may take risks when one knows when to do so. Sometimes taking risks pay off better than being too cautious. In other words, *The Prince* must be able to tell which risk is greater and act accordingly. One may attack now or later. The enemy is strong now, but they may get reinforcements later, and then they, too, are strong. So, it is better to attack now, although it is risky. If *The Prince* is used to quick and brash methods, this comes to him naturally. But the next time the situation may have changed. The reinforcements are not coming and the enemy troops are close to rebellion; one should wait a little longer before attacking. But it is difficult for *The Prince* who has always been quick, brash, and successful. Now he forgets the need to control his fortune. He still believes in the idea of coercing Fortune, but in this new situation it is a baneful strategy. He must wait. He must control himself, and by doing so, he can control his fortune. In this case, fortune is not an uncontrollable force nor is it just chance. Fortune is now a matter of careful calculations and self-control. In this way, one can eliminate the role of fortune in his own decisions and reach one's goals with a minimal uncertainty.

Luck, as minimal uncertainty, is en epistemic notion. *The Prince* is able to control his own fate by means of his *virtú* which is now something more than mere prowess. It is tried in battle and characterized by decisiveness, courage, and ruthlessness. Once one must deal with uncertainty, one must stop being a lion and become a cunning fox. As I said above, these two animals are mutually incompatible. The reasons for this are not so much psychological as they are semantic. If one is to be able to handle, successfully, such drastic uncertainty which *The Prince* meets in those political situations where conflicts are a life and death issue and in which no rules apply, one needs to be flexible. One needs to be a fox, and foxes flex the language. Too much decisiveness turns into a vice, an opposite of *virtú*. One needs stubbornness and deliberation. Instead of courage, one needs deceptiveness and slyness. Instead of ruthlessness, one may need compromise and forgiveness. *The Prince* must do what the situation demands and not what he is used to doing or what he is expected to do. He is at the mercy of the situation whose feature he cannot control. A lion could not manage it. A fox is needed. In this way, uncertainties can be countered by means of knowledge and know-how of the suitable responses and strategies. *The Prince* cannot be successful if he resorts to his customary ways of acting, his favorite attitude, and his traditional ways of behaviour. Now, the key word is flexibility.

Uncertainty is something one might be able to control, unlike the other forms of fortune. The reason is that uncertainty is an epistemic notion and therefore one is able to take countermeasures against it. When one is uncertain or when a situation contains uncertain elements, one should try to learn more about them and about the possible methods of reducing the uncertainties. This is possible, and once one has done his homework, the situation is less threatening and the risks of a disaster are under control. Yet this is a form of Fortune simply because whatever one does, the element of doom will never disappear completely. The residual of loss will remain, and this can be called bad luck. In this sense, one is always fighting against bad luck when one deals with uncertainty. But this kind of luck is controllable. Sometimes luck can be eliminated totally, for instance, when one decides not to act at all, nothing will happen, so there is no risk. In Machiavelli's cruel world, this is hardly a possibility. If there is one deterministic element in it, it is this: *The Prince* must act, and to act is to enter the world of uncertainties.

## NOTES

1. Machiavelli writes: "Time sweeps everything along and can bring good as well as evil, evil as well as good." (*The Prince*, tr. G. Bull, Penguin Books, Harmondsworth, p. 40). This aphorism entails fatalism, which may not look like Machiavelli's characteristic attitude.
2. See Machiavelli, *The Discourses*, ed. B. Crick and tr. L. J. Walker, Penguin Books, Harmondsworth, 1970.

3. The difference between cruelty and ruthlessness is all important when we discuss *virtú*. *The Prince* must not be cruel, otherwise he has no moral virtue, no honor, and he is not entitled to glory. It is unclear of this is means as an ethical statement or instrumental advice. Is the disvalue of cruelty intrinsic or extrinsic? Anyway, Machiavelli condemns cruelty, which entails excessive violence which is too dear to the perpetrator. He enjoys it. Ruthlessness is different as it means courageous determination. *The Prince* must do what is necessary to be successful, but he must respect certain limits. (See *The Prince*, ch. XVII) Yet the reputation for cruelty may sometimes be good (*The Prince*, p. 97). There is something tragic here: *The Prince* may need to be cruel but that stains his reputation. He has two possibly incompatible motives, namely, desire for glory and a mission to keep his principality alive.
4. *The Prince*, pp. 110 and 136.
5. *The Prince*, pp. 133–134.
6. Q. Skinner, Machiavelli, Oxford University Press, Oxford, 1981, p. 35.
7. Bull's Introduction to his translation of *The Prince*, p. 25.
8. G. Prezzolini, *Machiavelli*, tr. G. Savini, Robert Hale, London, 1967, p. 67–68.
9. S. de Grazia, *Machiavelli in Hell*, Princeton University Press, Princeton NJ, 1989, pp. 202–203.
10. *The Prince*, p. 136.
11. *The Prince*, p. 33.
12. *The Prince*, p. 133.
13. *The Prince*, p. 54 and p. 63.
14. Crick, Introduction to his edition of *The Discourses*, p. 61.
15. Yet Machiavelli writes: "...he could not have conducted himself other than the way he did..." (*The Prince*, p. 60). This is a nicely deterministic formulation.
16. In its simplest form it means a disaster: "You are bound to meet misfortune if you are unarmed..." (*The Prince*, p. 88).
17. *The Prince*, p. 130.
18. *The Prince*, p. 129.
19. *The Prince*, p. 60.
20. *The Prince*, p. 86–87.
21. *The Prince*, p. 123.
22. *The Prince*, p. 130–131.
23. *The Prince*, p. 132.
24. *The Prince*, p. 131.

Two

# BORDER-VALUE MORALITY AND SEMANTICAL COHERENCE IN MACHIAVELLI'S *PRINCE*

Hubert Schleichert

### Abstract

Machiavelli develops a morality that takes into account that he who wants to act is limited by other persons setting borders to his actions. The Prince is an answer to the problem how a politician should act if surrounded by "so many who are not good." Traditional moral theory very seldom deals with questions of that type. Although Machiavelli under certain conditions proposes shocking actions to rulers/politicians, he at the same time characterizes this actions as morally bad, making use of traditional moral terminology in its traditional meaning ("exceedingly bad, shame, injustice, detestable, fraud, contrary to humanity, repugnant"). He does not propose a morality for rulers, etc., different from that for ordinary people. Rulers (perhaps even Hegel's "world-historic individuals") are not placed outside everyday morality, even if they sometimes are forced to violate it. Such a position shows some structural similarity to Martin Luther's "pecca fortiter."

### "Absolute" Morality

A morality is a set of answers to questions of the type "What shall be done?", "What must not be done?", "How shall we act?"

Often answers to such questions are of a very simple logical and even grammatical form: "Do A!" or "Don't do B!". This is how morality is taught to children, or how morality is e.g. formulated in some of the commandments of the Old Testament: Don't kill! Don't steal! The rules are given without further explication, they are so to say context-free. They contain a "one ought..." without further specification, claiming to be valid in any situation whatsoever. They don't speak about how people on the average really act, and they don't take into account how other people in my neighbourhood would behave in reaction to my action. Therefore, one can call them "absolute."

The search for a few, very simple moral maxims that can be used as a guide in every and each situation is old.

"Is there a one-word principle that can be followed through whole life?", asked already a student his master Confucius (*Lun Yu* 15.24). He asked for a moral principle that is useful under all possible circumstances, in every situation of life.

A set of such principles, usually a small set, is called a system of morality. A person who sticks to these rules is called a good man, a person violating the rules is a bad man. As to the outcome of acting morally good, such an absolute system of morality does not say much. There are innumerable instances, in which sticking to an absolute morality works quite well and is a good instrument for peace-keeping in family and society. But this need not always be the case, and a just man often has to suffer a lot.

### Morality as a "Boundary-Value Problem"

I take the term "boundary-value problem" as an analogy from mathematics, meaning that the solution to a certain equation has to fulfil some additional requirements. With the help of these requirements, the solution can e. g. become the description of a concrete physical process, with concrete empirical data. In moral theory this means that one takes the given real situation into account when asking how to act. This is what Machiavelli does. Any kind of facts relevant for a decision or recommendation about how to act may generate a boundary-value problem. Acting in a morally relevant situation is always acting within a social world where other human beings react on my actions, set boundaries to my actions, and limit my possibilities. To ignore this fact can easily have catastrophic consequences.

The boundary condition Machiavelli is interested in most is the behavior and character of those, who are in one way or the other affected by my action. He first gives a description of what he considers as a basic fact about human behavior, especially (but not only) in the field of politics:

> One can generally say this about men: that they are ungrateful, fickle, simulators and deceivers, avoiders of danger, greedy for gain; and while you work for their good they are completely yours, offering you their blood, their property, their lives, and their sons, when danger is far away; but when it comes nearer to you they turn away. (*Prince*, ch. 17)

And he then draws the conclusion: "A man who wishes to profess goodness at all times will come to ruin among so many who are not good." (*Prince*, ch. 15)

This two sentences describe the boundary-value problem of political actions, as Machiavelli sees it.

The problem becomes now: How shall I act if surrounded by more or less bad, immoral people? To Machiavelli it is the basic moral problem of the politician in his struggle for power, but it can be taken as a more general question: to what extent should or must surrounding circumstances been taken into account in moral considerations? How shall a political leader act when the people are hard racists, extreme nationalists, or absolutely intolerant in religious matters, or have an old system of blood revenge, etc. This can set limits to even the most progressive and enlightened government, and may be used as justification for extraordinary actions. Other hard facts about human behaviour Machiavelli mentions are e. g. that people will never forget their hatred, or that the power of a prophet who has no weapons to force the people is limited, because people are not very stable in matters of belief, if there is no power that keeps them to that belief. (*Prince,* ch. 6)

There are a lot of empirical questions in Machiavellis approach: Is he right when giving such a pessimistic description of politicians or human beings in general? Is he right in his prognosis that, given the boundary-values as they are, a good man will necessarily come to ruin? But this is not my topic, and I shall assume that he is right. Thus, the question remains: How should a person act under circumstances as described by Machiavelli?

### Morality for Saints

The most simple answer is to ignore all limiting circumstances: Act along the lines of simple, unsophisticated morality, and don't care about the result. You will not necessarily be successful or have a happy life, but morality is on your side. He who practices justice and morality in many a case has to suffer a lot, including sometimes a miserable death. This is well known to every culture, and therefore in some cases such a person is called a saint or e.g., in classical moral-political Chinese philosophy, a nobleman (*junzi*).

The noble man, says Confucius, does his duty, and that morality (dào) will not always work is well known (*Lun Yu,* 18.6).

Some thinkers are more optimistic and state that with some effort one can always exert a positive influence on the people close to one, such that in the long run they change themselves into moral people, with whom one can negotiate according to the basic rules of morality. Classical Confucianism teaches that a ruler can influence his people simply through his personal moral (or, of course, immoral) example.

If you govern with correctness, who will dare not to be correct? told Confucius a ruler who asked about the right way to govern (*Lun Yu,* 12.17). Frederic II of Prussia, in his younger years Machiavelli's fervent critique, said the same, i. e., that people (including politicians) will be impressed by morally good actions and finally will respect the good man:

> Machiavel avance qu'il n'est pas possible d'être tout à fait bon dans un monde, aussi scélerat et aussi corrompu, sans périr. Et moi, je dis que pour ne pas périr, il faut être bon et prudent; alors le scélérats vous craindront et vous respecteront. (*Anti-Machiavel,* ch. 15)

This is an attempt to preserve simple, absolute morality and to neglect border-value problems, or, rather, to change the border-values. Put forward by a prince like Frederic II, unfortunately it sounds hypocritical. It is this way of treating morality, which Spinoza, one of the early readers of Machiavelli, called "a satire instead of a moral theory, that is of use at best... in a chimeric golden age of poets." (*Tract. Politicus* § 1) And it is of course not Machiavellis position.

Instead, he held a hard realistic view, when writing his famous statement

> ... among so many who are not good, ... it is necessary for a prince who wishes to maintain his position to learn not to be good, and to use this knowledge. (*Prince*, ch. 15)

This is his basic axiom for a ruler who is not a saint and does not want to loose power and life: he must learn to be bad.

### With or Without a Masque

It is not my intention to discuss if Machiavelli's axiom is *right*, although a lot of experience could back him up. I want, however, to underline two points in the structure of his theory. The first point of interest is that he refuses to work with absolute, context-free morality, including unrealistic illusions about how the moralist may change the feelings and behavior of people. The second point is that in formulating his basic axiom and in drawing conclusions from that axiom he does not change the meaning of moral terms. This is what I suggest to call his semantic coherence: What is called not good resp. bad in normal life, is called so also in Machiavelli's political philosophy.

In order to understand this better, we must distinguish between those parts of *The Prince* where Machiavelli speaks about how a prince should appear to the people, and parts where he speaks directly to a prince resp. to well informed, experienced members of the political upper class, who are his proper auditory. In the first case he shows how to wear a propagandistic masque, while in the second case he uses an open and very direct language.

For propagandistic reasons *The Prince* should wear a terminological masque and the hard facts be expressed in pleasing formulas, while the insider need not betray himself. *The Prince* was dedicated to one member of the Medici-family, i. e., for an insider. It was, told Machiavelli, his intention to write a thing which shall be useful to him who apprehends it ("a qui la intende"). (*Prince*, ch. 15)

Regarding the masses, e. g. in order to justify the breaking of a covenant, by *The Prince*, there will never be wanting to a prince legitimate reasons to excuse this non-observance...

But it is necessary to know well how to disguise this characteristic, and to be a great pretender and dissembler; and men are so simple, and so subject to present necessities, that he who seeks to deceive will always find someone who will allow himself to be deceived. (*Prince*, ch. 18)

A problem may arise, however, if a treatise written for insiders whom you can hardly provoke with open words is read by outsiders, i. e., the average people. As far as I can see, Machiavelli did not think much about this problem which later has been disturbing so many generations of his readers. In my opinion, part of the disturbance is due to the fact that he while giving shocking advices to rulers and politicians, still makes use of everyday moral terms with their standard meanings. Let me explain this by first giving a counterexample. The example can obviousely not be taken from Machiavelli.

**Splitting of Terminology: War as an Example**

To kill a human being is a murder. Murder has the worst possible moral evaluation. In war, innumerable human beings are killed; it is, however, never called murder or man slaughter but in every language gets different, quite peculiar names. If the killed people are from the other side, they have been annihilated or destroyed, it was our glorious victory, an elimination of a threat, an opening of a bright future, an event of world-historic importance, etc. If the killed are from our side, they are heroes who sacrificed their life for king and freedom. To kill in war is brave, and the more enemies a soldier kills, the greater will he be honored. But the very word is avoided – never call a brave soldier a killer or murderer!

Machiavelli noticed this splitting of terminology quite well when he, ironically, wrote:

> Although to use fraud in any action is detestable (detestabile), yet in the conduct of war it is praiseworthy and glorious ("laudabile e gloriosa"). (*Discorsi*, III. 40)

In fact, one finds a dramatic change of terminology when small-scale crimes like robbery or killing by single persons or small gangs are compared to large-scale actions of the same type, like conquest of a country or warfare in general. Very rarely does one hear that a state or an army has raided, robbed or stolen another country or territory, or that an army has murdered millions of soldiers or civilians. World history to a large extent is history of large-scale violence, and every language has special terms for such violence, giving it high-sounding patriotic names, especially when this violence has turned out to be successful. If one would keep to terminological coherence, such verbal tricks could not be used.

The incoherence of terminology, when large-scale fraud becomes praiseworthy, and detestable action becomes glorious, has already been pointed to in ancient China by the philosopher Mo Di in the fourth century B. C. In a vivid story he speaks about somebody who when seeing a small white spot correctly calls it "black," but calls huge black spots "white." This person obviously must have a perverted, distorted sensation; we would say, he is no longer clear about the meaning of terms. Now, to kill a man is called a crime, whereas to kill thousands during warfare is praised. This is how princes change the meaning of terms:

> If there were a man who, upon seeing a little blackness, should say it is black, but upon seeing much, should say it is white; then we should think he could not tell the difference between black and white... Now, when a little wrong is committed people know that they should condemn it, but when a great wrong, attacking a state, is committed people do not know that they should condemn it. On the contrary, it is applauded *and called* righteous... (*Mo Di*, ch. 17, Italics mine)

Already here it is indicated, that we have a distortion of terminology – something black/bad is *called* white/righteous.

At Machiavelli's time, war as such was something "normal" and not considered as a big moral problem. But even as he takes war as something regular and normal in politics, he describes it using basic moral terminology. In the *Discorsi* we read

> When on the decision to be taken wholly depends the safety of one's country, no attention should be paid either to justice or injustice, to kindness or cruelty, or to its being praiseworthy or ignominious. ("nè di giusto nè di ingiusto, nè di pietoso, nè di crudele, nè die laudabile, nè d'ignominoso") (*Discorsi*, III. 41)

As in war the safety of one's country is always at stake, war always means to forget justice, kindness, shame, etc. – warfare *is* unjust, immoral, bad and should be called so. But people don't like to be called by such terms. No ruler and no government will easily admit to be an aggressor, etc. – there will always be a pretense, a masque. In the words of Voltaire:

> L'idée de justice me paraît tellement une vérité du premier ordre, à laquelle tout l'univers donne son assentiment, que les plus grands crimes qui affligent la société humaine, sont tous commis sous un faux prétexte de justice. Le plus grand des crimes, du moins le plus destructif, et par conséquent le plus opposé au but de la nature, est la guerre; mais il n'y a aucun agresseur qui ne colore ce forfait du prétexte de la justice. [...]
> Le mot d'*injustice* ne se prononce jamais dans un conseil d'État, où l'on propose le meurtre le plus injuste. (*Le Philosophe ignorant,* ch. 32)

Machiavelli understands that it is a good trick to let the people believe in their leaders high wisdom and morality, and he is sure that this trick will work in most cases. But this is only one more of the practical tricks he describes for the insider: if necessary, betray people, tell them any lie about mass destruction weapons or whatever, and make a big show out of your honesty. Tell them that god is on our side! His book, however, is written for and dedicated to insiders, experienced politicians, and to these readers he can use an open, clear language and use terms according to normal usage.

## Beyond and Above Morality?

It is not unusual to ban all moral considerations from the field of political theory, and politics itself. Descriptions of historical phenomena don't gain much from additional moral commentaries. If what the acting individuals did was morally correct or bad, justifiable or not, can be left to other fields of study outside political history and theory.

In Hegels philosophy of history, however, this is much more than a simple methodological principle, it gets a metaphysical foundation. The more general our outlook on history and the more we conceive it as universal history, world-history, the less important become the "private" moral feelings of the acting persons. Finally, the "world-historic individuals" like Caesar or Napoleon (or Hitler, Stalin?) are simply beyond morality. World history takes place at a higher level than morality, and one must not bring forward moral claims against world-historic deeds and those who accomplish them (Hegel p. 90). And moral claims which are irrelevant must not be brought into collision with world-historical needs and their accomplishment. The litany of private virtues – modesty, humility, philanthropy, and fairness – must not be raised against them (Hegel, p. 91).

Some people think that to be also Machiavelli's position, but again they are not quite right. History to him is only history of human actions, not of abstract principles like Hegel's world-spirit. What human beings do, is always open to moral critique. In this, Machiavelli is much closer to real history. He could have easily avoided to mention moral conceptions completely. But in fact, exactly when he proposes something shocking, he inserts a short comment from the moral point. Princes, politicians, sometimes have to make decisions in extremely difficult situations, limited by various boundaries; if there is no other possibility, Machiavelli then recommends them even shameful actions. But he does not place them above moral judgement.

## Semantical Coherence

In his intercultural study on Machiavellism, Ben-Ami Scharfstein characterizes the difference between an anti-Machiavellist and a Machiavellist by saying that the first defends a morality with a single standard, while the second defends a moral standard for the ordinary person, and a different one for the state and state's leader. (Scharfstein, p. 5) In Scharfstein's opinion this difference can be found in several outstanding thinkers in Europe (namely Machiavelli), as well as in China, and India. But a careful reading of Machiavelli does not yield exactly this result.

To Machiavelli it *does* make sense to speak about morality in every field of action – we cannot and should not forget our moral basic standards, especially as we need them frequently many times in politics too. Unfortunately, however, under certain conditions it might be advisable to *act* against these moral standards, which he openly calls "immoral" or "bad" actions. This is his coherent use of standards and terminology. Machiavelli is shocking because he makes no use of semantic tricks. He takes the meanings of *good* and *bad*, of *moral* and *immoral* from everyday basic use of this terms and does not change their meaning. Words like "shame, cruel, to lie, steal, rob, murder," keep their meaning. In this he deviates from the usual terminology in politics and e.g. in the philosophy of history.

Machiavelli gives extraordinary maxims for extraordinary situations, but he does not change the meanings of *good* and *bad*. He recommends certain actions and at the same time calls these actions "exceedingly bad, cruel, repugnant" („crudelissimi o nemici d'ogni vivere," *Discorsi*, I. 26). If there is no other way, he says, be bad, be cruel, be immoral.

In chapter 15 he says:

"... it is necessary for a prince who wishes to maintain his position to learn not to be good, and to use this knowledge." (*Prince*, ch. 15)

And in the same chapter we read that *The Prince* need not hesitate to bear all shame ("infamia") for those vices without whom he would not have been able to save his power. (*Prince*, ch. 15)

This is called "Realpolitik" and is practised world-wide. Machiavelli is outstanding only in one point: he qualifies it as not good, as morally bad. His imperative is: If necessary, be bad. To follow this maxim, however, will never bring you glory, although on occasion it may win for you a state or kingdom. ("Dirò solo questo, che io non intendo quella fraude essere gloriosa, che ti fa rompere la fede data ed i patti fatti; perché questa, ancora che la ti acquisti, qualche volta, stato e regno, ... la non ti acquisterà mai gloria.") (*Discorsi*, III. 40)

The scandal is: he formulates the principles of "realistic politics" so extremely simple: It is shameful, it is bad – do it! While the traditional method always used semantic tricks, as Hobbes analyzed. Speaking about the violent (but, for the time being, successful) conquest of a state he notices a change of names and perversion of morality:

> Successful wickedness hath obtained the *name* of vertue: and some that in all other things have disallowed the violation of faith; yet have allowed it, when it is for the getting of a kingdom. (*Leviathan*, ch. 15, italics mine)

Machiavelli does not attack morality as a theory about good and bad, but states that given certain circumstances a prince should act in contradiction with morality, i. e., morally bad. The usual way, however, is to name by other terms the very same actions Machiavelli recommends under such conditions, like "efficient, prudent, statesman-like, according to historical necessity," etc., always tacitly presupposing, that they are morally good actions, or at least justifiable.

Machiavelli, however, gives them their usual names: *The Prince* should learn "not to be good," which obviousely means: bad. This moral statement is nowhere softened or neutralized by metaphysical constructions – *The Prince* is acting alone, he is not an executioner of world-spirit, world-reason, historic necessity or whatever.

To give one more example: Instead of speaking elegantly about a coup d'etat, Machiavelli says that rulership is sometimes successfully conquered by crime ("per sceleratezze," *Prince* ch. 8, headline), and makes it clear that one really cannot call murder of citizen, lack of humanity, etc. ("ammazzare li sua cittadini, tradire li amici, essere sanza fede, sanza pietà, sanza relligione") virtues, and that they will never bring honour, although eventually rulership over a state ("li quali modi possono fare acquistare imperio, ma non gloria," *Prince,* ch. 8).

In the same chapter, when speaking about bad or good use of cruelties, and explaining that "good use" means to perform all necessary cruelties *at once*, he adds: if it were allowed at all to call bad things good ("se de male è licito dire bene") and calls this a crime or injustice ("iniurie," *Prince*, ch. 8).

### Keeping One's Word

Perhaps the best known case is the question of fulfilling what one has promised. There is not much discussion between political philosophers and princes of all kind, that in real political life sometimes promises have to be ignored and acted contrary to what one has promised before. What is different, however, is the ideological interpretation. To Hobbes the definition of injustice, is no other than the not performance of covenant. (*Leviathan,* ch. 15)

Yet in the case of princes the words "just" and "unjust" cannot be applied, because states and their leaders live in "natural condition of war":

> But convenants of mutual trust, where there is a fear of not performance... are invalid... Injustice actually there can be none, till the cause of such fear be taken away; which while men are in the natural condition of war, cannot be done. Therefore before the names of just, and unjust can have place, there must be some coërcive power. (*Leviathan,* ch. 15)

Within Hobbes' political theory, states are always in a natural condition of war of anyone against any one, therefore a state resp. a prince has always a natural or rational right to do whatever he thinks to be necessary. So, not to fulfil promises between states is not shameful, is not morally bad, although under better circumstances it should not be done.

Machiavelli does not use such a theoretical construction; to him fulfilling of promises is good, and not fulfilling is bad. And sometimes we are forced to be bad. Even Machiavelli's fervent critic Frederic II admitted that there might sometimes be some necessity not to keep one's word:

> J'avoue d'ailleurs qu'il y a des nécessités fâcheuses où un prince ne saurait s'empêcher de rompre ses traités et ses alliances. Il doit cependant le faire de bonne manière en avertissant ses alliés à temps et non sans que le salut de ses peuples et une très grande nécessité l'y obligent. (*Anti-Machiavel,* ch. 18)

How one could not keep his word "in good manner" ("de bonne magniere"), remains open. The purpose of these words obviously is to make the sentence less shocking, to give it a smoother reading, to wear a terminological masque. Machiavelli, however, does not talk about "natural rights," or "good manner," he uses a direct language:

> A wise ruler cannot and should not keep his word when such an observance of faith would be to his disadvantage and when the reasons which made him promise are removed. If men were all good, this rule would not be good; but since men are all bad and wicked. ("Ma perché sono tristi," *Prince,* ch. 18)

Now, that princes of any genre throughout all times did not take their promises too seriously, is known only too well. The scandal is only that Machiavelli does not hesitate one second to speak it out in everyday, vulgar terminology. He refuses to participate in the game of verbal camouflage.

### Pecca Fortiter

I have tried to analyze the structure of Machiavelli's thought from a methodological point, or, to be exact, from the point of moral theory. The structure of a moral system with strict terminological coherence or consistency can be seen with special clarity in the field of politics. In principle, however, it is a universal structure with many possible applications. There are many situations in human life as a social being where it is difficult or practically impossible to follow strictly the lines of basic morality, as one feels them immediately.

To torture is definitely bad and should never be done, never. Yet, if there is, e. g., a kidnapper who does not tell where he has locked up his victim, and we are sure, the life of his victim is in danger – a lot of us would be prepared to torture him until he gives the information needed. Machiavelli's description of the situation would be: "To torture is terribly bad, and if it is the only way to safe an innocent life, than do it!" To rob a person's purse is theft; if it is done by a very large company, stealing the pensions of thousands of pensioners or shareholders, those who do it should be openly named and treated as criminal thieves, not as businessmen who made use of possibilities in the world of business. They should be forced to confess: "Theft is a crime, and we are thieves!" But let me turn to a more general consideration.

Also to religious leaders the fact is quite well known, that in real life it is often impossible to act stictly along the line of basic morality, or, in religious terminology, to act without sin. The more decisions one has to made, the more one can (or must?) perhaps deviate from a morally or religious good life.

Now there is a famous sentence by Machiavelli's contemporary Martin Luther, namely:

Esto peccator et pecca fortiter sed fortius fide! Be a sinner and be brave in sinning, but even braver in your faith. (Luther letter 424)

The sentence was written in a letter to Melanchthon from 1521, only about 6 years later than the composition of *The Prince*.

Luther's short remark, taken out from its original context, is sometimes quoted when one is going to act in a somehow not quite correct manner, violating fundamental religious rsp. moral principles, but seemingly unavoidable: Be brave in your actions and don't hesitate, do what must be done, even when it is sinful! Humans that we are, we cannot always keep our hands clean. At the same time be faithful and firm in your belief, and finally you will be saved and get the eternal life.

Not every theologician agrees with this interpretation; some take it as deep religious wisdom, others for terrible heresy (see e. g. Grisar, Vol. 2, p. 158–161). According to this last interpretation, Luther tells his followers to do whatever sinful they like, if they so please, relying on god's immense mildness and grace – exactly as traditional critics have interpreted Machiavelli. The difference is only, that Machiavelli obviously does not care at all about eternal blessedness but much about power.

The friendlier interpretation, however, ist also quite similar for Luther and Machiavelli. It entails, of course, that one should try to be morally or religious as perfect as possible, to lead a life without crime or sin. One should always try his best. Only, you have to know that the surrounding world may set limits to your effort to be good. In that case be prepared to do what is necessary, even if it is bad resp. a sin. But you must know, that it is bad or sinful. As long as we are on earth, we must sin; this world is not the place of justice.

Peccandum est, quandiu hic sumus; vita haec non est habitatio iustitiae, sed expectamus coelos novos et terram novam, in quibus iustitia habitat. As long as we are here we must sin: this world is not the place of justice. But we are expecting a new haven and a new earth, where justice resides (Luther, ibid.) as Luther writes. Like Machiavelli, Luther here is terminologically coherent. What is a sin, a peccatum, is called a sin in every context – and unfortunately must be done often enough in this world. So if you can't avoid sin, don't have too many scruples, don't hesitate, commit the inevitable sins without delay: sin bravely and don't try to hide behind semantic tricks from the fact that you sinned.

In the same mood Machiavelli writes:

And you have to understand this, that a prince, especially a new one, cannot observe all those things for which men are esteemed, being often forced, in order to maintain the state, to act contrary to fidelity, friendship, humanity, and religion. Therefore it is necessary for him to have a mind ready to turn itself accordingly as the winds and variations of fortune force it, yet, as I have said above, not to diverge from the good if he can avoid doing so, but, if compelled, then to know how to set about it. („non partirsi del bene, potendo, ma sapere intrare nel male, necessitato", *Prince,* ch. 18)

Once again he makes use of normal every-day moral terms in their standard meaning: it might be acting against fidelity, humanity and religion, it might be something very bad, something "male." He did not claim particular standards of good and evil for the ruling class, differing from those for the people. The difference, to him, is, that the ruler may be forced to do something morally bad, "necessitato intrare nel male."

In practical life, the difference between Machiavellians and Antimachiavellians, like (in that respect) Lutherans and Antilutherans, vanishes, but in the interpretation of life, in self-justification or ideology the difference remains, and it seems, that here Machiavelli is on the honest side.

# WORKS CITED

*Anti-Machiavel* (by Frederic II, published anonymously, edited by Voltaire): *The Complete Works of Voltaire,* Vol. 19, Oxford 1996.
*Confucius* (Lun Yu), transl. by J. Legge *The Four Books,* repr. New York 1966.
Grisar, Hartmann, S. J.: *Luther,* 3 vols. Freiburg 1911.
Hegel, G.W.F., *Vorlesungen über Philosophie der Geschichte*; Werke in 20 Bänden, suhrkamp 1970, Bd. 12.
Hobbes, Th.: *Leviathan or the matter, form, and power of a commonwealth,* 1651.
*D. Martin Luthers Werke, Briefwechsel* Bd. 2, Weimar 1931, repr. 1969. The letter to Melanchthon is from August 1st, 1521 (nr. 424, = pg. 370–373).
*The Ethical and Political Works of Motse,* transl. Mei Yi-Pao, London 1929.
Scharfstein, Ben-Ami: *Amoral Politics, The Persistent Truth of Machiavellism,* State University of New York Press, 1995.
Spinoza, *Tractatus Politicus.*
Voltaire, *Le Philosophe ignorant,* Complete Works of Voltaire, vol. 62, Oxford 1987.

# Three

# NICCOLÒ MACHIAVELLI ON POWER*

Manfred J. Holler[1]

Altobello Melone, *Portrait of Cesare Borgia*

**Abstract**

This paper uses the concept of power to analyze Machiavelli's *The Prince* and *The Discourses on the First Ten Books of Titus Livius*. This helps to distil the elements that form the Machiavelli program that has its short-term aim in the formation of a national state of Italy. A unification of Italy under the umbrella of a princely family (such as identified with Cesare Borgia) was meant to be the first stage in an evolutionary process which, in the end, could lead to a more or less stable republican system. For the latter, the Roman Republic as described in *The Discourses* is Machiavelli's model. The use of power, but also the minimization of cruelties, and the participation of the people, either in the form of militia to successfully fight foreign armies or to support the princely government, are major ingredients to this process.

"A few years ago, I'd read *The Prince* and I liked it a lot. Much of what Machiavelli said made sense, but certain things stick out wrong – like when he offers the wisdom that it's better to be feared than loved, it kind of makes you wonder if Machiavelli was thinking big. I know what he meant, but sometimes in life, someone who is loved can inspire more fear than Machiavelli ever dreamed of." (Dylan, 2005, p. 140f)

### Introduction

*The Prince has no power.* This is the immediate consequence of applying Weber's seminal concept of power to Machiavelli's *The Prince* as we will see below. Of course, this conclusion seems highly paradoxical since Niccolò Machiavelli has been praised and condemned as prophet of unconstrained power. It seems that there is more to power in Machiavelli's writings as common understanding and superficial interpretation suggest. In this paper I scrutinize *The Prince*

---

* A significantly modified version of this paper was published as Holler, Manfred J. (2009), "Niccolò Machiavelli on Power," in: M. Baurmann and B. Lahno (eds.), *Perspectives in Moral Science. Contributions from Philosophy, Economics, and Politics in Honour of Hartmut Kliemt*, Frankfurt: Frankfurt School Verlag, 335–354. Permission to reprint is granted by Frankfurt School Verlag.

and *The Discourses* with the concept of power hoping to get a deeper insight in Machiavelli's political and philosophical ideas. My expectation is that the reader will concur with what I suggest to be "the Machiavellian" program.

To bring the discussion into focus the paper takes off with an outline of the Machiavellian program. Section 2 restates the issue of power in Machiavelli's political writings. Section 3 examines these issues using various definitions of power, using Weber's concept of power as a litmus test. Various aspects of power, such as balance of power, autonomous power, and the power of the sword, are reviewed in Sections 4 and 5. Section 6 is a short summary, some challenging remarks, and my conclusions.

## 1. The Machiavelli Program

The central thesis of this paper is that the Roman Republic of 16th century Italy was the target of Machiavelli's political writings envisaging a united national state. There are straightforward indicators of this in *The Prince*. In finalizing Chapter 26, Machiavelli directly addresses the governing Medici to whom he dedicates his text:

> It is no marvel that none of the before-mentioned Italians have done that which it is hoped your illustrious house may do. (*The Prince*, p. 125),

and

> May your illustrious house therefore assume this task with that courage and those hopes which are inspired by a just cause, so that under its banner our fatherland may be raised up... (ibid., p. 107)

Regardless, the unification of Italy under the umbrella of a princely family is just a first step in the Machiavelli program. As I will show below, unification is meant to be the first stage in an evolutionary process which, in the end, could lead into a, more or less stable, republican system.

Machiavelli dedicated the text of *The Prince* to Lorenzo the Magnificent, son of Piero di Medici.[2] This dedication has been interpreted as Machiavelli's attempt to gain the favour of one of the powerful Medici "in the hope that they might invite him back to public service" (Gauss, 1952, p. 11). This interpretation seems to be widely accepted and probably contains some truth. In the context of Machiavelli's program, however, the dedication can (also) be interpreted as a second attempt of initiating the creation of a united Italy under the rule of the Medici, guaranteeing peace and order.

In a letter to his friend Francesco Guicciardini, Machiavelli suggested the Condottiere Giovanni de'Medici as the liberator of Italy.[3] This was years after Machiavelli saw Cesare Borgia failing in his project to conquer substantial shares of Italy and to resist the claims and the power of the vassals and followers of the French and Spanish Crown and of the German Emperor who divided Italy as spoils of war.

Machiavelli maintained that, despite rather skilled precautions, Cesare Borgia was defeated by *fortuna*. It was *fortuna* which brought about the early death of Cesare Borgia's papal father Alexander VI. And again, it was *fortuna* who blinded him when he supported the election of Julius II as successor of his father. Instead of being a supporter to his ambitious projects, Julius II turned out to be a rival to the power himself.

The Machiavellian program becomes evident when one compares Roman history as interpreted in *The Discourses* with the facts that one learns about Cesare Borgia as selected in *The Prince*. In both cases there is an extremely cruel beginning in which the corresponding "heroes" violate widely shared norms of the "human race." It has been argued that Machiavelli's choice of Cesare Borgia, also called the *Duke*, to become the hero of *The Prince* was a grave error from the standpoint of his later reputation as "Cesare had committed crimes on his way to power, and it might be added that he had committed other crimes too." (Gauss, 1952, p. 12f)

It seems that Machiavelli anticipated such a critique, and consequently

> Reviewing thus all the actions of the Duke, I find nothing to blame, on the contrary I feel bound, as I have done, to hold him up as an example to be imitated by all who by fortune and with the arms of others have risen to power. (*The Prince*, p. 57)

Here again the Machiavellian program is shining through. Whoever has the power should follow the path outlined by Cesare Borgia – and by Romulus. Concerning the status and evaluation of crimes in this program, Romulus, mythic founder of Rome, even killed his brother Remus in order not to share power. He also "consented to the death of Titus Tatius, who had been elected to share the royal authority with him" (*Discourses*, p. 120). In the interpretation of Machiavelli, these murders guaranteed that one (and only one) will define the common good. It was the will of *The Prince*.[4]

It is important to note that for Machiavelli Cesare Borgia's cruelties and Romulus's fratricide *were* violations of moral norms. However, as is notoriously quoted, Machiavelli accepted that the violation of moral norms can have its justification: "...in the action of men, and especially of princes, from which there is no appeal, the end justifies the means." (*The Prince*, p. 94)

The period of cruelties and "destructive purification"[5] was meant to be followed, in the case of both Rome and the unified Italy, by peace and order that presupposed protection from external enemies. Thus, "destructive purification" was to the benefit of the people. In the Roman case, the giving of law by *The Prince* was a major component to support peace and order. In a more mature state, this princely phase was followed by the division of power together with the introduction of a republican order.

In the case of Cesare Borgia, the project ended with the early death his father, Pope Alexander VI. Cesare's powerbase became too weak to continue the project of transforming the Papal State into a Borgia State and of extending the Borgia State for all Italy, so to have enough power to keep foreign governments and armies out of the country.

In the case of Romulus and Rome, history went on to the evolution of the Roman Republic. Machiavelli gave an (efficiency) argument why, in the end, the princely government is expected to transform into a republican system as the governmental regime stabilized. In Chapter IX of *The Discourses* one reads: "...although one man alone should organize a government, yet it will not endure long if the administration of it remains on the shoulders of a single individual; it is well, then, to confide this to the charge of many, for thus it will be sustained by the many."

As we know from history, and stated in *The Discourses*, in the case of Rome the transformation into a republic was not a peaceful event. Yet, Machiavelli's belief in Republics to be the most stable political system becomes obvious from his writings. The costs in taking political systems by force and to establish a princely power are likely to be prohibitive compared to capture of power in a principality. "...in republics there is greater life, greater hatred, and more desire for vengeance; they do not and cannot cast aside the memory of their ancient liberty, so that the surest way is either to lay them waste or reside in them." (*The Prince*, 1952, p. 47)

Both alternatives, one should add, are perhaps not too profitable. It should be noted that Machiavelli has seen the Republic of Florence taken over by the Medici without experiencing much resistance after the Florence militia disintegrated in the Battle of Prato, at the hands of Spanish infantry. The fact that the Medici decided to "reside in it," does however not contradict Machiavelli's theory. Contrariwise, the case illustrates that the republican spirit in Florence was not very strong. This is consistent with Machiavelli's interpretation.

Yet, there is another efficiency argument in favour of the republic: it offers a possibility to get the people involved in government. In Chapter 58 of Book I of *The Discourses*, Machiavelli gives a series of arguments why he thinks that "the people are wiser and more constant than princes" (p. 214) if their behaviour is regulated by law. If his arguments hold then a state that allows for the participation of the people is preferable to principalities which are dominated by a single despot, a king of divine right, or a small clique of nobles. However, the participation of the people does not exclude the possibility of the emergence of a despot and the transformation of a republic into tyranny. Machiavelli gives several examples for this possibility and the case of Rome is the most apropos. The latter demonstrates the importance of adequate laws and institutional rules to prevent individual citizens from capturing power. Machiavelli argues that if "we study carefully the conduct of the Roman republic," we discover that "the prolongation of her military commands" was one of the two reasons "of her decadence." (*Discourses*, p. 387)

For the farther the Roman armies went from Rome, the more necessary did such prolongation of the military commands seem to the Senate, and the more frequently did they practise it. Two evils resulted from this: militarization. The first was that fewer men became experienced in the command of armies, and therefore distinguished reputation was confined to a few. The other was that by the general remaining a long while in command of an army, the soldiers became so attached to him personally that they made themselves his partisans, and, forgetful of the Senate, recognized no chief or authority but him. It was thus that Sylla and Marius were enabled to find soldiers willing to follow their lead even against the republic itself. And it was by this means that Cæsar was enabled to make himself absolute master of his country." (*Discourses*, p. 388)

Machiavelli neither was quite aware that efficiency argument as such neither guarantees that a republic prevails nor save a republic, if it exists, from the decay into a princely state, tyranny or anarchy.

It is reasonable to surmise that, had it become reality and matured like Rome did, Machiavelli hoped that the Borgia Italy finally would transform to a republic,. It seems quite obvious from the final chapter in *The Prince* that Machiavelli wanted to talk the Medici into another attempt to accomplish the project of an all-Italian state that is strong enough to guarantee peace and order for its citizens, and to fight foreign enemies.

In his "Introduction to *The Prince*," Christian Gauss writes:

Machiavelli had spent thirteen years in earnest striving to improve the lot of his country, and learned much that is revealing and valid. His reward was exile. It is idle to deny that *The Prince* is a bitter book. Its bitterness is the result of his failure in his time. The modern reader cannot afford to allow this to blind him to what it contains which is still valid for our days. (1952, p. 30)

I cannot concur that *The Prince* is a bitter book. Gauss himself described it as a "handbook for aspirants to political power" (ibid., p. 12). It seems that this political power is not self-contained, but it can be identified as part of Machiavelli's program to better Italy's destiny and thus "improve the lot of this country." Contrary to Gauss, this is an optimistic perspective. The handbook is meant to be a tool to develop this power which is a necessary prerequisite for peace and order. Hence, given that he had no public position after the fall of Piero Soderini in 1512, it can be interpreted as an alternative way how Machiavelli could have served his country.

It could be argued that there is conflict between the progressive structure of the Machiavelli program, as outlined here, and the circular view which Machiavelli holds on history: there is growth and prosperity followed by destruction, chaos and possible reconstruction; princely government is followed by tyranny, revolution, oligarchy, again revolution, popular state, and finally the republic which in the end collapses into anarchy waiting for *The Prince* or tyrant to reinstall order. (See *Discourses*, p. 101)

Also, in Machiavelli's *History of Florence* one can read:

> The general course of changes that occur in states is from condition of order to one of disorder, and from the latter they pass again to one of order. For as it is not the fate of mundane affairs to remain stationary, so when they have attained their highest state of perfection, beyond which they cannot go, they of necessity decline. And thus again, when they have descended to the lowest, and by their disorders have reached the very depth of debasement, they must of necessity rise again, inasmuch as they cannot go lower. (*History*, p. 218)

Machiavelli concludes:

> Such is the circle which all republics[6] are destined to run through. Seldom, however, do they come back to the original form of government, which results from the fact that their duration is not sufficiently long to be able to undergo these repeated changes and preserve their existence. But it may well happen that a republic lacking strength and good counsel in its difficulties becomes subject after a while to some neighbouring state, that is better organized than itself; and if such is not the case, then they will be apt to revolve indefinitely in the circle of revolutions. (*Discourses*, p. 101f)

The above quote is an indication that the "circle" is no "law of nature" although the image is borrowed from nature.[7] There are substantial variations in the development of the governmental system and there are no guarantees that the circle closes again. Obviously, there is room for political action and constitutional design that has a substantial impact on the course of political affairs. For instance, Machiavelli concludes that "…if Rome had not prolonged the magistracies and the military commands, she might not so soon have attained the zenith of her power; but if she had been slower in her conquests, she would have also preserved her liberties the longer." (*Discourses*, p. 388)

Accordingly, despite his circular view of the world, Machiavelli considered political action and constitutional design highly relevant to the course of history and also to what happens today or tomorrow. However, the circular view allows us to learn from history and apply what we learned today in the future. Machiavelli repeatedly urges his contemporaries to study the Romans and to learn from them. In fact, in can be argued that Machiavelli wrote *The Discourses* to serve mainly this purpose.

In the next sections details of Machiavelli's program are clarified. The focus is on power and the status it has in both *The Prince* and *The Discourses*. As I will show it is not always obvious what the status of power is and how substantial power is to various agents.

## 2. The Issue of Power

One would be hard pressed to find a better illustration of power in Machiavelli's Prince than in the episode concerning how Cesare Borgia made use of his minister Messer Remirro de Orco to gain power and to please the people:

> When he [Cesare Borgia] took the Romagna, it had previously been governed by weak rulers, who had rather despoiled their subjects than governed them, and given them more cause for disunion than for union, so that the province was a prey to robbery, assaults, and every kind of disorder. He, therefore, judged it necessary to give them a good government in order to make them peaceful and obedient to his rule. For this purpose he appointed Messer Remirro de Orco, a cruel and able man, to whom he gave the fullest authority. This man, in a short time, was highly successful, whereupon the duke, not deeming such excessive authority expedient, lest it should become hateful, appointed a civil court of justice in the centre of the province under an excellent president, to which each city appointed its own advocate. And as he knew that the hardness of the past had engendered some amount of hatred, in order to purge the minds of the people and to win them over completely, he resolved to show that if any cruelty had taken place it was not by his orders, but through the harsh disposition of his minister. And having found the opportunity he had him cut in half and placed one morning in the public square at Cesena with a piece of wood and blood-stained knife by his side. The ferocity of this spectacle caused the people both satisfaction and amazement." (*The Prince*, p. 55)

If one analyzes this episode with respect to power one can interpret Cesare Borgia's behaviour as a successful solution of a strategic (game theoretical) problem: how to bring order to the Romagna, unite it, and reduce it to peace and fealty, without being made responsible for the necessary cruelties, and thus the creation of hate. Machiavelli claims that cruelty was necessary, or at least, in modern parlance, a socially efficient solution. (*The Prince*, p. 55) It is worth noting that it is the combination of cruelty with legal procedures that helps to transform cruelty to a common good.

This episode demonstrates that the power of Cesare Borgia depended on his skills of strategic thinking and, one must admit, on the naivety of his minister. Messer Remirro de Orco could have concluded that the *Duke* will exploit his capacity; and in the very end this capacity included that he had to serve as a sacrifice to the people who *had* to suffer cruelties to *enjoy* the fruits of a strong government and order.

Perhaps Messer Remirro de Orco saw himself and the *Duke* in a different context and the game that reflected this context did not propose the trial and his death as an optimal alternative to the *Duke*.[8] Obviously, the misfortune of Messer Remirro de Orco was that the *Duke*'s game was based on the offering of an "officer" to the consolation of the people. It seems that the *Duke* was quite aware that the love of the people may prevent conspiracies from within and serves as a rampart to outside competitors (see, e. g., *The Prince*, pp. 96 and 108), or in fact serve in both roles.[9]

Game theoretic thinking seems apropos here. Strategic thinking is a dominant feature in Machiavelli's writings and the thinking of his "agents." Machiavelli, thus, could well be considered as a pioneer of modern game theory. It does not come as a surprise that the language of this theory straightforwardly applies to the core of Machiavelli's analysis.

If the interpretation of Messer Remirro de Orco's misfortune is valid here then one must conclude that the power of the Duke is highly dependent on historical circumstances, political constraints and his strategic skills. In fact, Max Weber's definition of power allows one to judge that he had no power at all since he was not in a position "to carry out his own will despite resistance."[10] On the other hand, Cesare Borgia was a master to circumvent resistance and, finally, to achieve most oh his goals.

For instance, as Cesare Borgia feared that a successor to Pope Alexander VI might seek to take away from him what he had gained under his father's papal rule, he destroyed "all who were of blood of those ruling families which he had despoiled, in order to deprive the pope of any opportunity" (*The Prince*, p. 56). This example demonstrates that Borgia did not accept a given resistance as constraint to his power, but would try to overcome it. The relationship of power and constraint is discussed in more detail in the next section.

In Machiavelli's *Discourses*, power of the Roman Republic derives from
(a) The recognized duty of the citizens concerning the common good,
(b) The law which specifies the duty, and
(c) Political institutions that implement the duty in accordance to the law and revise the law in accordance to the duty.

Free states are those "which are far from all external servitude and are able to govern themselves according to their own will."[11] A strong military organization is the indispensable pillar. Only if it exists, citizens can hope "to live without fear that their patrimony will be taken away from them, knowing not merely that they are born as free citizens and not as slaves, but that they can hope to rise by their abilities to become leaders of their communities."[12]

This statement links the individual freedom of not being a slave and the external freedom of the community, the free state, and to participating in the shaping of the political actions of this community, i. e., the potential to play an active and effective role in political life. However, Machiavelli points out that free citizens are generally reluctant to serve the common good and prefer to pursue their own immediate advantage. In game theoretical terms: free-riding is a dominant strategy. That is where the law and political institutions step in to overcome this dilemma. "It is the hunger of poverty that makes men industries and it is the laws that make them good."[13]

The law however could be corrupted by the biased interests of various groups or by prominent members of the community. This problem is solved, by-and-large through adequate political (and/or religious) institutions. "...under their republican constitution," the Romans had one assembly controlled by the nobility, another by the common people, with the consent of each being required for any proposal to become law. Each group admittedly tended to produce proposals designed merely to further its own interests. But each was prevented by the other from imposing its own interests as laws. The result was that only such proposals as favoured no faction could ever hope to succeed. The laws relating to the constitution thus served to ensure that the common good was promoted at all times.[14]

The common good seems to be identifiable with a compromise between the two major political agents. The Coase Theorem tells us that bargaining between two agents produces an efficient outcome if
(a) Property rights are well defined, and
(b) Transaction costs are zero, even when there are externalities (Medema and Zerbe, 2000).

Unfortunately, it is difficult to think of a real world case with zero transaction costs. Thus, efficiency is not assured and the parties can find arguments to improve the organization of the State by shaping it in accordance with their biased preferences. The installation of the *decemviri* (from 451 to 449 BC), discussed in more detail below, is just one case that demonstrates the fragility of the compromise on which the Roman Republic was built.

## 3. On Power

Machiavelli is often seen as a predecessor of Thomas Hobbes.[15] Obviously, their views on human nature and the function of the authority of the state have much in common. To some extent they also share the fate that their writings were not highly appreciated for quite some time and even today they meet with strong reservations.

As Machiavelli, neither in *The Prince* nor *The Discourses*, offers any explicit definition of power, it seems to be right to start to analyze the state of power in Machiavelli's work with a reference to Hobbes' famous opening sentence of Chapter 10 of the *Leviathan*: "[t]he power of a man is his present means, to obtain some future apparent good."[16]

Hobbes does not restrict himself to choices of social interaction. Power in Hobbsian theory is a far broader concept than social power. But, if we think of power in terms of chances to affect results social power is a special case. It is unclear, though, whether power should be restricted to obtain some future apparent "good." If so, then Hobbes' definition links the concept of power to preferences of an actor.

Perhaps power should rather be conceived as any ability to intervene into the course of the world regardless of the preferences we espouse with respect to results of action. Quite a bit depends here on how one interprets the term "apparent" and how one specifies the very concept of preference. It seems that the application of Hobbes' concept of power raises more questions than it allows one to find answers, though it might come the closest to the spirit that fuels Machiavelli's work. However, Machiavelli talked about power only in the political or social context. He was not interested in (nonhuman) nature unless it was related to "man." For instance, Machiavelli maintains that *The Prince* must "learn the nature of the land, how steep the mountains are, how the valley debouch, where the plains lie, and understand the nature of rivers and swamps" so that one can "better see how to defend it." (*The Prince*, p. 82)

Weber's concept of social power seems to be a straightforward restriction of the Hobbesian concept of power (as a potential) to social contexts.[17] It says: "Macht bedeutet die Chance, innerhalb einer sozialen Beziehung den eigenen Willen auch gegen Widerstreben durchzusetzen, gleichviel worauf diese Chance beruht" (Weber, 2005[1922], p. 38). Notwithstanding the very plausible interpretation of the Weberian "Chance" as meaning "chance," Talcott Parsons translated this famous passage as: "the *probability* that one actor within a social relationship will be in a position to carry out his own will despite resistance." (Weber 1947, p. 152, italics added). However, in *Essays from Max Weber*, edited by Hans H. Gerth and C. Wright Mills, we read: "In general, we understand by 'power' the *chance* of a man or of a number of men to realize their own will in a communal action even against the resistance of others who are participating in the action" (italics added). This is the translation of Weber's definition given on page 678 of *Wirtschaft und Gesellschaft*. (Weber (2005[1922], p. 678)[18]

Given this definition, the dilemma of fear and love which is implicit in Machiavelli's writings becomes obvious. As I have shown Machiavelli argues that the love of the people may prevent conspiracies from within and serves as a rampart to outside competitors. However, a prince who makes use of this potential is dependent on the people. His range of goals which he can achieve "despite resistance" will be small if he has to be afraid to lose the support of the people and perhaps even provoke resistance. It seems that Machiavelli himself was aware of this dilemma when he raised the question "whether it is better to be loved more than feared, or feared more than loved" (*The Prince*, p. 90). His answer is: "I conclude, however, with regard to being feared and loved, that men love at their own free will, but fear at the will of *The Prince*, and that a wise prince must rely on what is in his power and not what is in the power of others, and he must only contrive to avoid incurring hatred, as has been explained" (*The Prince*, p. 91). This conclusion fits well with the concept of power proposed by Weber but neglects the strategic advantages that *The Prince* can derive if he succeeds to be loved by the people at a not too high price, or by the sacrifice of dispensable companions like Messer Remirro de Orco.

The conflict between a favourable dependency and the autonomy of power characterizes Machiavelli's work. This is a consequence of the strategic thinking which he excessively proposes to the heroes of his writings. If you put yourself into the shoes of others, you become dependent on what they think and what you expect them to do, if you do not have a dominant strategy in your quiver. However, strategic thinking could enlarge your set of possibly successful actions.

Reputation is a possible consequence of strategic thinking. The reputation qualities of *The Prince* are the expectations of those who put themselves into the shoes of *The Prince*. It is straightforward that a "good reputation" is a means for successful government. *The Discourses* are filled with numerous examples. However, reputation can also be used to mislead people and to exploit them when necessary.

Machiavelli points out that for a prince "...it is well to seem merciful, faithful, humane, sincere, religious, and also to be so; but you must have in mind so disposed that when it is needful to be otherwise you may be able to change to the opposite qualities" (*The Prince*, p. 93). Not surprisingly Machiavelli concludes that it "... is not, therefore necessary for a prince to have all the above-mentioned qualities, but it is very necessary to seem to have them. I would even be bold to say that to possess them and always to observe them is dangerous, but to appear to posses them is useful" (*The Prince*, p. 93). Sentences like this, although largely supported by empirical evidence, are the source of Machiavelli's "bad reputation" over the centuries, especially, of course, with those who had princely power (like Fredric II of Prussia who has written *Anti-Machiavelli* in his younger years) or served princely power (like William Shakespeare).

What can be said about the power of an individual in the republic?

> ...the Roman republic, after the plebeians became entitled to the consulate, admitted all its citizens to this dignity without distinction of age or birth. In truth, age never formed a necessary qualification for public office; merit was the only consideration, whether found in young or old men. ... As regards birth, that point was conceded from necessity, and the same necessity that existed in Rome will be felt in every republic that aims to achieve the same success as Rome; for men cannot be made to bear labour and privations without the inducement of a corresponding reward, nor can they be deprived of such hope of reward without danger. (*Discourse*, p. 221)

And admitting that this may be so with regard to birth, then the question of age is necessarily also disposed of; for in electing a young man to an office which demands the prudence of an old man, it is necessary, if the election rests with the people, that he should have made himself worthy of that distinction by some extraordinary action. And when a young man has so much merit as to have distinguished himself by some notable action, it would be a great loss for the state not to be able to avail of his talents and services; and that he should have to wait until old age has robbed him of that vigour of mind and activity of which the state might have the benefit in his earlier age. (*Discourses*, p. 222)

Again one finds a strong efficiency argument. In principle, though, individual power in the Roman Republic has its source in much the same circumstances as the power of the *Duke* in Renaissance Italy, however constrained by law and political institutions that are to implement the common good. Yet, if these constraints do not work the results are quite similar. It is perhaps not a coincidence that the founding of Rome follows a pattern that could be designed by Cesare Borgia. As already mentioned, Romulus "should first have killed his brother, and then have consented to the death of Titus Tatius, who had been elected to share the royal authority with him." (*Discourses*, p. 120)

Machiavelli admits that "from which it might be concluded that the citizens, according to the example of their prince, might, from ambition and the desire to rule, destroy those who attempt to oppose their authority" (*Discourses*, p. 120). However,

> ... this opinion would be correct, if we do not take into consideration the object which Romulus had in view in committing that homicide. But we must assume as a general rule that it never or rarely happens that a republic or monarchy is well constituted, or its old institutions entirely reformed, unless it is done by only one individual; it is ever necessary that he whose mind has conceived such a constitution should be alone in carrying it into effect. A sagacious legislator of a republic, therefore, whose object is to promote the public good, and not his private interests, and who prefers his country to his own successors, should concentrate all authority in himself; and a wise mind will never censure any one for having employed any extraordinary means for the purpose of establishing a kingdom or constituting a republic. (*Discourses*, p. 120)

This sounds like a blueprint and a justification for the cruelties initiated or committed by the Duke. We should not forget that both the stories of Cesare Borgia and Romulus were told by the same author. It seems however that Romulus was more straightforward and less constrained in his use of force than the *Duke* who was by-and-large limited to the use of "strategic power."

Notoriously, superficially and slanderously as well, Machiavelli's contribution is often summarized by his view that the justification for the use of power, however cruel, derives from its ends. In the case of Romulus, Machiavelli concludes: "It is well that, when the act accuses him, the result should excuse him; and when the result is good, as in the case of Romulus, it will always absolve him from blame. For he is to be reprehended who commits violence for the purpose of destroying, and not he who employs it for beneficent purposes." (*Discourses*, p. 120f)

Except there is no guarantee that the will of the founding hero to do the public good carries over to the successor. The creation of an appropriate law is one way to implement the pursuance of the public good. Consequently, Machiavelli proposes that the "lawgiver should... be sufficiently wise and virtuous not to leave this authority which he has assumed either to his heirs or to any one else; for mankind, being more prone to evil than to good, his successor might employ for evil purposes the power which he had used only for good ends." (*Discourses*, p. 121)

### 4. The Balance of Power

An alternative or complementary device to implement the pursuance of the public good is the *division of power* and the subsequent cooperation of the various stakeholders:

> ...although one man alone should organize a government, yet it will not endure long if the administration of it remains on the shoulders of a single individual; it is well, then, to confide this to the charge of many, for thus it will be sustained by the many. Therefore, as the organization of anything cannot be made by many, because the divergence of their opinions hinders them from agreeing as to what is best, yet, when once they do understand it, they will not readily agree to abandon it. That Romulus deserves to be excused for the death of his brother and that of his associate, and that what he had done was for the general good, and not for the gratification of his own ambition, is proved by the fact that he immediately instituted a Senate with which to consult, and according to the opinions of which he might form his resolutions. And on carefully considering the authority which Romulus reserved for himself, we see that all he kept was the command of the army in case of war, and the power of convoking the Senate. This was seen when Rome became free, after the expulsion of the Tarquins, when there was no other innovation made upon the existing order of things than the substitution of two Consuls, appointed annually, in place of an hereditary king; which proves clearly that all the original institutions of that city were more in conformity with the requirements of a free and civil society than with an absolute and tyrannical government. (*Discourses*, p. 121)

This quote demonstrates the implementation of power relations via institutions such as the law and the division of power. Basically, these institutions constrain individual decision making and determine the freedom of choice. Under these constraints, the participation of various groups in lawmaking and political decision making ends up either in competition and possible conflict, or in bargaining and consent. As already argued, under a few and rather restrictive assumptions, bargaining leads to an efficient outcome which can be identified as the common good.

Obviously, Machiavelli was far ahead of his time in his support of balance of power. His point of departure is the empirical observation and theoretical insight that

> ... all kinds of government are defective; those three which we have qualified as good because they are too short-lived, and the three bad ones because of their inherent viciousness. Thus sagacious legislators, knowing the vices of each of these systems of government by themselves, have chosen one that should partake of all of them, judging that to be the most stable and solid. In fact, when there is combined under the same constitution a prince, a nobility, and the power of the people, then these three powers will watch and keep each other reciprocally in check. (*Discourses*, p. 101)

The Roman Republic has all three elements: nobility and people as its natural components and the princely positions of consuls, tribunes and, in case of a crisis, dictators that derive from its natural components through bargaining, voting, deliberation and other procedures of collective decision making. However, this balance of power did not always work. In the end, the Roman Republic was the prey of despots the like of Marius, Sulla and, finally, Julius Caesar, although even before those the balance of power was under attack in the Roman Republic. For instance, in Chapter 40 of Book I of *The Discourses*, Machiavelli tells us the story of the Decemvir Appius who gained the power to act as a despot.

In 451 BC, the *Decemviri* were established as a result of a severe conflict between the people and the nobility. More and more the people were inclined to think that the ongoing wars with Rome's neighbours were a plot by the nobility to discipline and suppress them. As consuls were the head of the various armies the people started to hate this institution. According to Machiavelli, the people hated the title of consul more than the power which derives from this position. The election of tribunes with the function of consuls seemed to be a way out of the dilemma, but this solution was unacceptable to the nobility. After some time the institution and name of consul was re-established and the conflict became more sincere than ever. A new constitution seemed to be the only way to solve this conflict, but there was no institution that was authorized and considered as sufficiently neutral to accomplish the necessary reform.

After many contentions between the people and the nobles respecting the adoption of new laws in Rome, by which the liberty of the state should be firmly established, it was agreed to send Spurius Posthumus with two other citizens to Athens for copies of the laws which Solon had given to that city, so that they might model the new Roman laws upon those. After their return to Rome a commission had to be appointed for the examination and preparation of the new laws, and for this purpose ten citizens were chosen for one year, amongst who was Appius Claudius, a sagacious but turbulent man. And in order that these might make such laws irrespective of any other authority, they suppressed all the other magistracies in Rome, and particularly the Tribunes and the Consuls; the appeal to the people was also suppressed, so that this new magistracy of ten became absolute masters of Rome. (*Discourses*, p. 182)

The *Decemviri* had despotic power and Appius Claudius was most prominent member of the Ten. When the Sabines and the Volscians declared war on Rome, two armies under the command of several *Decemviri* left the city. Appius, however, remained in order to govern the city.

It was then that he (Appius) became enamoured of Virginia, and on his attempting to carry her off by force, her father Virginius killed her to save her from her ravisher. This provoked violent disturbances in Rome and in the army, who, having been joined by the people of Rome, marched to the Mons Sacer, where they remained until the Decemvirs abdicated their magistracy, and the Consuls and Tribunes were re-established, and Rome was restored to its ancient liberty and form of government. (*Discourses*, p. 184f)

In his analysis of this historical event, Machiavelli argues that here we must note that the necessity of creating the tyranny of the Decemvirs in Rome arose from the same causes that generally produce tyrannies in cities; that is to say, the too great desire of the people to be free, and the equally too great desire of the nobles to dominate. And if the two parties do not agree to secure liberty by law, and either the one or the other throws all its influence in favour of one man, then a tyranny is the natural result. The people and the nobles of Rome agreed to create the Decemvirs, and to endow them with such great powers, from the desire which the one party had to destroy the consular office, and the other that of the Tribunes. (*Discourses*, p. 185)

As a consequence the balance of power, on which the functioning of the Republic was built, was destroyed becoming dysfunctional. However, the expectations of the various parties were foiled, too.

Having created the Ten, it seemed to the people that Appius had come over to them and would aid them to keep the nobility down, and therefore they supported him. Now when a people goes so far as to commit the error of giving power to one man so that he may defeat those whom they hate, and if this man be shrewd, it will always end in his becoming their tyrant. For with the support of the people he will be enabled to destroy the nobility, and after these are crushed he will not fail in turn to crush the people; and by the time that they become sensible of their own enslavement, they will have no one to look to for succour. This is the course which all those have followed who have imposed tyrannies upon republics. (*Discourses*, p. 185)[19]

Tyranny was not a necessary the result of an evolutionary process, but the consequences of political errors. It seems obvious that Machiavelli discusses the case of Appius to show to future generations the consequences of these errors and to teach them what has to be avoided in order to protect their freedom.

Both the Senate and the people of Rome committed the greatest errors in the creation of the Decemvirate; and although we have maintained, in speaking of the Dictator, that only self-constituted authorities, and never those created by the people, are dangerous to liberty, yet when the people do create a magistracy, they should do it in such a way that the magistrates should have some hesitation before they abuse their powers. But the people of Rome, instead of establishing checks to prevent the Decemvirs from employing their authority for evil, removed all control, and made the Ten the only magistracy in Rome; abrogating all the others, because of the excessive eagerness of the Senate to get rid of the Tribunes, and that of the people to destroy the consulate. This blinded them so that both contributed to provoke the disorders that resulted from the Decemvirate. (*Discourses*, p. 186f)

## 5. Autonomous Power

The Weberian definition of power is based on the degree of autonomy of the decision maker. According to this perspective the more dependent the decision maker is on the support of others, the smaller is his degree of power. This also applies to an agent who has the strategic capacity to manipulate his social environment in order to reduce or eliminate resistance, as Cesare Borgia did, so that he can have his will. It seems that in Renaissance Italy autonomous power of any substance can only be enjoyed under the strong umbrella of the church. Ecclesiastical principalities ... are acquired either by ability or by fortune; but are maintained without either, for they are sustained by ancient religious customs, which are so powerful and of such a quality, that they keep their princes in power in whatever manner they proceed and live. These princes alone have states without defending them, have subjects without governing them, and their states, not being defended, are not taken from them; their subjects not being governed do not resent it, and neither think nor are capable of alienating themselves from them. Only these principalities, therefore, are secure and happy. (*The Prince*, p. 69)

Over a substantial period, the Popes and their Kingdom of Rome also benefited from "old religious customs." Yet, the spirit of the Renaissance not only inspired secular princes and their competitors but also the persons in the succession of Saint Peter. Sixtus IV (1471–1484) is said to strongly support the venture to murder Lorenzo Magnifico and his brother Giuliano when the two attended a mass at the Cathedral of Santa Maria del Fiori. Lorenzo escaped wounded but his brother was stabbed in the heart. Almost ironically, although not a reparation, a natural son of Giuliano became a papal successor of Sixtus IV by the name of Clement VII.

Before Clement VII took office, there were other rather worldly Renaissance popes. Alexander VI's "object was to aggrandise not the Church but the duke" (*The Prince*, p. 70) as Cesare Borgia was his son. Much what can be said about the actions of the *Duke* can therefore also be related to his father. However, under the umbrella of "old religious customs" the Pope seemed to demonstrate special qualities of strategic behaviour. Machiavelli reports that he "did nothing else but deceive men, he thought of nothing else, and found the occasion for it; no man was ever more able to give assurance, or affirmed things with strong oaths, and no man observed them less; however, he always succeeded in his deceptions, as he well knew this aspects of things." (*The Prince*, p. 93)

As successful and exploitive this policy was, it is questionable whether it could be called "autonomous" as it largely depended on the trust the Pope enjoyed by those with whom he interacted. Deceptive behaviour is strategic because it presupposes that a player puts himself into the shoes of the other. However, the fact that the Pope was not weakened by his deceptive behaviour in his potential to deceive others, demonstrates some autonomy, probably because of his papal position.

The papal position, the historical conditions, and his martial personality, seemed to allow Julius II to act "impetuously in everything he did...that he always obtained a good result" (*The Prince*, p. 122). In the first war that Julius II waged against Messer Giovanni Bentivogli's Bologna he "achieved what no other pontiff with the utmost prudence would have succeeded in doing, because, if he had waited till all arrangements had been made and everything settled before leaving Rome, as any other pontiff would have done, it would never have succeeded" (*The Prince*, p. 122). It appears that Julius II seemed to play his game, irrespective of what other players thought or did; he acted autonomously. He was successful because the circumstances were in his favour, and not because his capacity was unconstrained by any means. "...had time followed in which it was necessary to act with caution, his ruin would have resulted, for he would never have deviated from these methods to which his nature disposed him." (*The Prince*, p. 122)

It is obvious from Machiavelli's writings that he did not think highly of ecclesiastical principalities and the papal state. The latter he saw as a major barrier to the unification of Italy. Part of Machiavelli's dissatisfaction with these particular entities has to do with their lack of sensitivity to the political needs and demands of the citizens and the neighbouring states, i. e., the autonomy of their power.

## 6. Conclusions

In this paper it was not argued that *The Discourses* present a model for a community where one sees virtue and virtuous lawgivers that guarantee peace and order – and protection from outside enemies. This is the standard interpretation. I suggest that *The Discourses* are a model of the political process that Machiavelli hopes for and tries to initiate by his writing to see a united Italy, strong enough to fight its outside enemies. It has been argued that Cesare Borgia was the wrong hero to choose. However, there was no better alternative in his time to highlight the envisioned political development. The like of Romulus were far and few. In fact, there is a very close similarity between Romulus and Cesare Borgia when it comes to the use of power and how they acquired it. But fortuna was with former and not with the latter. I have conjectured that *The Prince* was meant to bring the Medici to the forefront to accomplish this project.

It is interesting to note that Machiavelli does not expect a collective to be strong and well-organized enough to bring about a united Italy or powerful Rome. He repeatedly argues that it needs a single will (and fortuna) to create a powerful entity that can successfully resist outside enemies and provide peace and order. By-and-large collectives play a rather passive role. They can support *The Prince* or fight him. In Chapter 40 of Book I of *The Discourses* Machiavelli maintains that "those tyrants who have the masses for friends and the nobles for enemies are more secure in the possession of their power, because their despotism is sustained by a greater force than that of those who have the people for their enemies and the nobles for their friends." (p. 186)

In the Roman Republic, the people seemed to have more power. They succeeded to install the tribunes and to reduce the position of the consuls. In the case of the Decemvir Appius the people even exerted immediate power. However, throughout Machiavelli's writings the people have no face and no name; rather they have the form of "masses" as in preceding quotation. Nothing is said how collectives organize themselves and how they exert power if not by marching to the Mons Sacer.

If one thinks that this is a shortcoming for someone considered to be the father of modern political science, then I must stress that by assuming strategic reasoning for the political agents and the deductive method of explanation Machiavelli was way ahead of his time. Many political scientists are still hesitant towards the application of game theory to political problems, and deductive arguments are still considered a *Glasperlenspiel* by many in the profession. The very same people often complain about the scientific imperialism of the economists who indeed share Machiavelli's way of thinking, but not necessarily the subject.

The structural interpretation of the question "whether it is better to be loved more than feared, or feared more than loved" (*The Prince*, p. 90) is familiar to economists, but, until recently, its subject could not be found in textbooks or mainstream journals of economics. During the last decade, however, research about happiness became popular in economics and love and fear are considered in this context. Even more frequently economists speak about ends and means, but they hardly ever discuss the ends. In economics, the question whether "the ends justify the means" (*The Prince*, p. 94) is not a question to be answered.

To conclude, Machiavelli was not an economist, and many political scientists are quite hesitant to see him as a forerunner of political science. Was he, then, a philosopher? Perhaps the following quote from the Fifth Book, Chapter I of his *History of Florence* may help to answer this question:

...when brave and well-disciplined armies have achieved victory, and victory has produced peace, the vigour of warlike spirits cannot be enervated by more honourable indulgence than that of letters; nor can idleness enter any well-regulated communities under a more alluring and dangerous guise. This was perfectly well understood by Cato when the philosophers Diogenes and Carnedes were sent as ambassadors from Athens to the Senate of Rome; for when he saw the Roman youth begin to follow them with admiration, Cato, well knowing the evil that would result to the country from this excusable idleness, ordered that no philosopher should thenceforth be received in Rome. (*History*, p. 218)

# WORKS CITED

Arrow, Kenneth J. (1963), *Social Choice and Individual Value*, New York: John Wiley and Sons.

Dylan, Bob (2005), *Chronicles: Volume One*, New York et al.: Simon & Schuster.

Gauss, Christian (1952), "Introduction to the MENTOR Edition" of Niccolò Machiavelli, *The Prince*, New York: Mentor Books.

Hobbes, Thomas (1651/1991), *Leviathan*, edited by Richard Tuck, Cambridge: Cambridge University Press.

Holler, Manfred J., Hartmut Kliemt, and Hannu Nurmi (2006), "Actions and Acts in Game and Decision Theoretic Accounts of Power," (unfinished manuscript).

Kersting, Wolfgang (2006), *Niccolò Machiavelli*, 3rd ed., Munich: Verlag C. H. Beck.

Machiavelli, Niccolò (1952), *The Prince*, New York: Mentor Books.

Machiavelli, Niccolò (1882), *Discourses on the First Ten Books of Titus Livius*, in: *The Historical, Political, and Diplomatic Writings of Niccolò Machiavelli*, translated from the Italian by Christian E. Detmold, in Four Volumes, Boston: James R. Osgood and Co.

Machiavelli, Niccolò (1882), *History of Florence*, in: *The Historical, Political, and Diplomatic Writings of Niccolò Machiavelli*, translated from the Italian by Christian E. Detmold, in Four Volumes, Boston: James R. Osgood and Co.

Machiavelli, Niccolò (1977), *Discorsi. Gedanken über Politik und Staatsauffassung*, translated and edited by Rudolf Zorn, 2. ed., Stuttgart: Alfred Kroener Verlag.

Medema, Steven G. and Richard O. Zerbe, Jr. (2000), "Educating Alice: Lessons from the Coase Theorem," *Research in Law and Economics* 19, 69–112, p. 80.

Skinner, Quentin (1984), "The Paradoxes of Political Liberty," The Tanner Lectures on Human Values. Delivered at Harvard University, October 24 and 25.

Weber, M. (1947), *The Theory of Social and Economic Organization*, edited by T. Parsons, New York: Free Press.

Weber, M. (1948[1924]), "Class, Status and Party," in: H. H. Gerth and C. Wright Mills (eds.), *Essays from Max Weber*, London: Routledge and Kegan Paul.

Weber, M. (2005[1922]), *Wirtschaft und Gesellschaft. Grundriß der verstehenden Soziologie*, Zweitausendeins: Frankfurt am Main.

Zorn, Rudolf (1977), *Einleitung* zu N. Machiavelli, *Discorsi. Gedanken über Politik und Staatsauffassung*, 2. ed., Stuttgart: Alfred Kroener Verlag.

## NOTES

1. Institute of Socioeconomics, University of Hamburg, Von-Melle-Park 5, D-20146 Hamburg, holler@econ.uni-hamburg.de. – The author would like to thank Matthew Braham, Leonidas Donskis and George Frankfurter for very helpful comments.
2. Lorenzo the Magnificent is the grandson of Lorenzo di Medici who died in 1492 and entered history books as *The Magnificent*. His grandson died in 1519, too early to fulfil Machiavelli's aspirations. However, it is not evident that the "new" Lorenzo ever read Machiavelli's text. (See Gauss, 1952, p. 11)
3. Francesco Guicciardini later became the highest official at the papal court, and first commander of the Pope's army. Guicciardini remained Machiavelli's friend until the latter's death. Nevertheless, Guicciardini didn't often support Machiavelli's plans and ideas. (See Zorn, 1977, pp. XXXVIIf and LIX)
4. If this will is consistent and strong enough to fight inside and outside rivals, then peace and order prevails. Relating this view to Arrow's Impossibility Theorem seems straightforward (see Arrow, 1963). Arrow demonstrates that a consistent and complete ranking of social state can only be guaranteed if it concurs with the preferences of a rational individual, i.e., dictator, independent of the preferences of other individuals in the very same society.
5. As I have written these lines at the Indira Gandhi Institute of Development Research at Mumbai I have to point out that "destructive purification" is one of the characteristics of the God Shiva.
6. The German translation is „die Regierungen aller Staaten "(Machiavelli, 1977, p. 15), i. e., "the governments of all states," which is perhaps more adequate than to address the republic only.
7. Kersting (2006, p. 61ff) contains arguments that imply that Machiavelli relied much stronger on the circle principle than I propose here. Human nature does not change. It wavers between selfish creed and ruthless ambition, on the one hand, and the potential to strive for the common good, on the other. Depending on the state of the world, one finds that the one or the other inclination dominates in frequency and success. There is also the possibility of the "uomo virtuoso" who, supported by fortuna, will lead his people out of the lowlands of anarchy and chaos. The result of this potential and the alternative inclinations is a cyclical up-and-down which sees tyranny and free state as turning points but still contains enough leeway for the formative power of virtue and fortuna.
8. Seen in isolation, the *Duke*'s offering of Messer Remirro de Orco, although a successful move was not even part of a subgame perfect equilibrium of this game as it presupposed a non-rational behaviour of the second player. Messer Remirro de Orco should have considered that Cesare Borgia could be tempted to use him as a scapegoat.
9. In Chapter 40 of *The Discourses*, Machiavelli argues that "the support of the people his internal forces suffice to sustain" a tyrant. This "was the case with Nabis, the tyrant of Sparta, when he was assailed by all Greece and the Romans; he made sure of the few nobles, and having the people his friends he succeeded in defending himself by their aid, which he never would have been able to do had the people been hostile to him."
10. For Max Weber's definition of power, see section 3 below.

11. I. ii. p. 129 of Niccolò Machiavelli (1960), Il Principe e Discorsi, ed. Sergio Bertelli (Milan Felrinelli), translated by Quentin Skinner. See Skinner (1984, p.239).
12. Ibid., II. ii. p. 284 (see Skinner, 1984, p. 240).
13. Ibid., I. iii. p. 136 (see Skinner, 1984, p. 244).
14. This is how Skinner (1984, p. 246) summarizes Machiavelli's description of the law making institutions of the Republic.
15. Zorn (1977, p. LXVI) argues that Machiavelli is of much higher importance than his "vielüberschätzter Schüler Hobbes" (i. e., his "overvalued pupil Hobbes"). To both, without the supremacy of the power of the state, life is brutish, cruel and short. Hobbes seems to prefer monarchy, while Machiavelli is in favour of the republic. However, in Machiavelli the form of government is not a matter of choice but the result of an evolutionary process. In this circular process, tyranny and anarchism have their necessary functions.
16. Hobbes (1651/1991), p. 62.
17. The Hobbes-Weber comparison of power is discussed in a work in progress by Holler et al. (2006).
18. The possibility not withstanding that Parsons simply misunderstood the Weberian concept, or committed some blunder in translation due to negligence, there seems to be a deeper issue here concerning the very nature of power itself: An outside observer of social interaction could in her account of power indeed try to rely exclusively on the probability that certain results will be brought about rather than on the potential to bring them about. But this "probability" interpretation will not do justice to the notion of her own power an actor would endorse herself. (See, Holler et al., 2006)
19. And if Appius had done the same, his despotism would have had more vitality, and would not have been overthrown so quickly; but he did exactly the reverse, and could not have acted with more imprudence. For to hold his despotic authority he made himself the enemy of those who had given it to him, and who could have maintained him in it; and he equally made himself the friend of those who had in no way contributed to it, and who could do nothing to keep him in it; and he ruined those who were his friends, and sought to make those his friends who never could become so. For although it is the nature of the nobility to desire to dominate, yet those who have no share in such domination are the enemies of the tyrant, who can never win them all over to him, because of their extreme ambition and avarice, which are so great that the tyrant can never have riches and honours enough to bestow to satisfy them all. And thus Appius, in abandoning the people and allying himself with the nobles, committed a manifest error, both for the reasons above stated, and because, to hold a government by violence, it is necessary that the oppressor should be more powerful than the oppressed (*Discourses*, p. 185f).

Four

# THE MODERN WHO BELIEVED THAT HE WAS THE ANCIENT: NICCOLÒ MACHIAVELLI IN EUROPEAN THOUGHT AND POLITICAL IMAGINATION

Leonidas Donskis

### 1. The Genesis of the Modern Individual

A modern identity-concealment-and-revelation game, a sophisticated variety of hide-and-seek, this phenomenon comes into existence together with the emergence of individualism. Italian, Flemish, Dutch, and German Renaissance masters start signing their canvases, thus signifying the arrival of the Era of the Individual; yet they play identity games that become part of the picturesque carnival of the language and artistic expression. Instead of signing their given and family names, they drop a hint or leave a mark as if to say that the identification of the master is an inescapable part of the interpretation of the work of art itself.

An identity concealment leaving part of the clue to that identity is a metaphor of the modern identity game that calls for affirmation of existence: I exist insofar as you identify me as a person; say my name, and bow to me as a Unique Individual on the Face of the Earth. I begin existing as an individual only when you identify me and my artwork, which is my silent autobiography. The deeply symbolic and allegoric nature of Renaissance and Baroque art invites and incites a viewer, an eyewitness of being, to experience a joy of revelation, deciphering hidden meanings and allusions. Like an allusion or allegory, our identity is just a mask covering the face of being. Like a search for an original and unique means of expression or an authentic artistic language, which always remains an effort, our moral choices bring us closer or, on the contrary, distance us from others. Grasp of life and understanding of the other is a continuous path to our own moral substance. If we put it aside, our self becomes merely a mask, a game, and a joke for the sake of amusement of merry ladies and gentlemen.

*Als ich kan* (as well as I can) is a recurring motto by, and a clue to identification of, the author that appears on paintings by Jan van Eyck. The portrait of the Arnolfini couple, a powerful proof of the miracle of the face of the individual, contains this motto, which allows us to identify Van Eyck's existential and aesthetic traces there. We hasten to read two letters, RF (*Rembrandt fecit*, the Latin abbreviation for "Rembrandt executed this work of art") just to make sure that we stand before Rembrandt himself, and not his pupils Ferdinand Bol, Aert de Gelder, or Carel Fabritius. Of Rembrandt's *De Nachtwacht (The Night Watch)* Oswald Spengler, in *Der Untergang des Abendlandes*, wrote as frozen history. Therefore, a great work of art, in addition to its ability to remind us of the mystery of being and the individuality of every human face, body, object of reality, thing, or any other trace of being, allows us a point of entry into history.

That art can reveal not only concealed identities and frozen history but also untold stories we learn from Raphael's *Portrait of Pope Leo X* (1518–1519). We know that Raphael (Raffaello Sanzio, 1483–1520) executed this magnificent work just a year before his death. More than that, one of the two Cardinals standing behind the Pope, both relatives and cardinal-nephews of Leo X, Luigi de' Rossi (ca. 1471/74–1519) died shortly after this work saw the light of the day. Another Cardinal, a member of the Medici family just like the Pope himself, Giulio de' Medici (1478–1534), later succeeds Leo X as Pope Clement VII. Scholars suggest that that the scene represents Leo X and his cousin Giulio de' Medici listening to the sentence of 4 July 1517 that condemned the Sienese Cardinal Alfonso Petrucci (ca. 1490–1517) to death for plotting to kill the Pope.

The accusation of Petrucci for his conspiracy and high treason, as well as his execution, appears to have been not a big consolation before the fate of their all, though. Pope Leo X, born Giovanni de' Medici (1475–1521), passed away two years after Raphael immortalized him in a group portrait with two Cardinals. Last but not least, in spite of the Pope's power and prestige, it was the beginning of the time of trouble for the Papacy and the Church, as Martin Luther dealt a blow to their standing and international reputation. In addition, Clement VII broke with Henry VIII and England because of his unsanctioned and illegitimate divorce from Katherine of Aragon. What do we have here? A prophetic vision of a great artist? Or a blend of secret, conspiracy and mystery uniquely concentrated in a group of influential individuals portrayed by Raphael?

Raphael did not need his great mastery and creative genius to make an intrigue here. We will always remain indebted to a great master for the mystery of the individuality of a human face – especially when this mystery is sharpened by our knowledge that we observe the face of a dying or otherwise passing individual. The secret behind the scenes is sufficient to strengthen the mystery of the power of Raphael's masterpiece's appeal. A blend of secret and mystery, Alfonso Petrucci's alleged conspiracy creates the initial disposition of power exercised by the Pope and two Cardinals in great solemnity.

Like any other power game and part of covert narrative, conspiracy is tailor-made for a work of art. It contains a mystery while offering a secret: something promised to be revealed, yet another segment of covert narrative structure to be kept unexposed. Conspiracy fuels our historical and political imaginations. They had long been, and will continue to be, part of art. Even putting aside the conspiracy theory of society both as a cognitive phenomenon and as an aspect

*The Modern Who Believed that He Was the Ancient:
Niccolò Machiavelli in European Thought and Political Imagination*

Raphael, *Pope Leo X with Cardinals Giulio de' Medici and Luigi de' Rossi*

of power structure and its interpretation, it remains obvious that it is always linked to secrets and mysteries as covert aspects of social reality. This makes the conspiracy theory serve as an unmistakable source of success for any kind of sensationalist literature and journalism. It is an indispensable element of what is supposed to be an exciting literary plot that offers secrets or mysteries as semi-public and semi-private properties of modern individuals and societies. As such, it is likely to survive into the centuries to come.

Yet the conspiracy theory would not have become one of the major plots and traits of the modern moral imagination had it been not developed as a mode of discourse within the framework of political thought. Curiously enough, this mode of discourse coincides and even overlaps with something far more fundamental in modern Europe – namely, the genesis of the self-asserting, self-sufficient, reflective, and brave individual capable of bridging thought and action. Like in William Shakespeare's *Hamlet*, this emergence of the individual can signify the marriage of thought and action. *La mente audace*, that is, the brave mind – this ideal put forward by Renaissance humanists is obvious in Hamlet's ability to outsmart and get rid of his treacherous friends Rosencrantz and Guildenstern. Yet the arrival of the modern individual may signify the reverse tendency, the divorce of thought and action, which is the case with Hamlet, and which becomes the reason of his defeat – albeit political, rather than moral – and death.

No thinker has ever embodied and represented these, one would think, mutually exclusive facets of modern individualism as Niccolò Machiavelli.

## 2. The Great Riddle of Niccolò Machiavelli

Recently, a noticeable flurry of attempts in the academic literature has reinterpreted Niccolò Machiavelli's (1469–1527) personality and body of work, which had been demonized for so long that the historical and actual Machiavelli has been transformed into a figure we might describe as similar to a modern-age equivalent of the Woland character in Mikhail Bulgakov's novel, *The Master and Margarita* (written in 1928–1941, and published, severely censored, in 1966–1967).

If we refer only to Machiavelli's small book, entitled *The Prince*, which was intended as a means of ingratiation with the Medici dynasty who ruled Florence in his day, then perhaps some basis exists for such an assertion (see White, 2005; Berlin, 1979, 25–79). All those who have shown an interest in the ideas of this strange and mysterious diplomat, writer, and thinker, will likely recall his notable lion and fox metaphors along with the counsels he proffered in *The Prince*: if you cannot rely on force and act like a lion, become a fox and act with stealth. In truth, Machiavelli was a thinker of far greater complexity than the scheme of his pamphlet may reveal. As Florence's ambassador to France living in Paris, Machiavelli understood perfectly the constant threat posed to a fragmented and divided Italy by powerful centrally governed states, by France, in particular.

As a Florentine patriot, as a humanist in the truest sense, and as someone who believed in the ideals of the Roman Republic, Machiavelli dreamed of a perfect political organism that was incorruptible, un-poisoned, and un-manipulated, which would grasp and then master the entire technology of power along with the repertoire of palace intrigue so that once it had taken root in Florence and spread quickly through all of Italy, it could recreate within it a civilized social and moral order, a republican order. If you doubt this, then read *Discorsi sopra la prima deca di Tito Livio* (*Discourses on Livy*, written between 1513 and 1521, and published in 1531), Machiavelli's work on politics that is of far greater importance than *The Prince*.

Machiavelli secretly admired the appalling treachery, manipulation, cruelty, and cynicism of Cesare Borgia, the son of the famous Pope Alexander VI and the head of the papal army who became a cardinal at the age of twenty-two and later a general. This entire nightmare of nepotism and corruption was possible thanks to the political practices of the Spanish nobleman Roderic Borja, who became Pope Alexander VI in a move that was a serious blow to the reputation of the Church.

Yet Machiavelli admired Cesare Borgia, this dangerous beast, who was a danger to him. Cesare was close to Machiavelli's political and educational ideal of *The Prince* instructed by the teacher who would be *un mezzo bestia e mezzo*

## The Modern Who Believed that He Was the Ancient: Niccolò Machiavelli in European Thought and Political Imagination

*uomo* (half beast, half man). Machiavelli understood quite well that only someone of the ilk of Cesare could put an end to papal political omnipotence, while putting an end to the untrammeled political banditry of a dysfunctional state, and thereby create a strong centralized state similar to France or Spain.

Some politicians and nobles were shocked by *The Prince* when it was first published. Others thought that Machiavelli was simply cataloguing the behavior of all politicians in a candid way but without affixing labels. Still other interpreters of Machiavelli guessed that he was a satirist and was poking fun at immoral politics while maintaining a facade of seriousness and respect. Incidentally, many other Renaissance humanist writers had done similar things; consider Machiavelli's contemporary, Sir Thomas More's *Utopia* (1523), and Erasmus of Rotterdam's *Encomium Moriae* (*Praise of Folly*, 1509).

Whatever the case, no one was so disgusted by Machiavelli as the great English poets and dramatists of the Elizabethan era, especially Christopher Marlowe and William Shakespeare. In the prologue to Marlowe's play, *The Jew of Malta*, Machiavelli, as if he were the very incarnation of Satan, is made to say the following:

> Albeit the world thinks Machiavel is dead,
> Yet was his soul but flown beyond the Alps;
> And now the Guise is dead, is come to France,
> To view this Land, and frolic with his friends.
> To some perhaps my name is odious,
> But such as love me guard me from their tongues;
> And let them know that I am Machiavel,
> And weigh not men, and therefore not men's words.
> Admired I am of those that hate me most.
> Though some speak openly against my books,
> Yet they will read me, and thereby attain
> To Peter's chair: and when they cast me off,
> Are poisoned by my climbing followers.
> (Cited in Cassirer, 1974, 119)

In Shakespeare's historical drama, *Henry VI* (Part Three, Act 3, Scene 2), Richard, Duke of Gloucester, says:

> Why, I can smile and murder whiles I smile,
> And cry Content to that which grieves my heart,
> And wet my cheeks with artificial tears,
> And frame my face to all occasions.
> I'll drown more sailors than the mermaid shall;
> I'll slay more gazers that the basilisk;
> I'll play the orator as well as Nestor,

>Deceive more slily than Ulysses could;
>And, like a Sinon, take another Troy.
>I can add colours to the chameleon,
>Change shapes with Proteus for advantages,
>And set the murderous Machiavel to school.
>(Ibid., 118)

The story of Machiavelli's interpretation and demonization is a long and tortuous one, worthy of a separate course in university political science departments. In the nineteenth century, Machiavelli was especially demonized by the French antimonarchists, who associated the restoration of Napoleon III with Machiavelli's nefarious cunning. During the twentieth century, Machiavelli was knocked about by historians and political scientists studying the history of the rise to power of Stalin and Hitler and their régimes, based as they were on overt political banditry.

The Bolsheviks were beginning to be referred to as Machiavellians. This version was popularized by Arthur Koestler, the British writer of Hungarian origin, in his *Darkness at Noon* (1940). We should consider James Burnham in this context. Burnham's book, *The Managerial Revolution* (1941), had a great impact on George Orwell, who also considered as Machiavellians the virtuosos of the twentieth century's brutal *Realpolitik*.

The Carbonari, Italy's nineteenth-century patriots, began openly admiring Machiavelli. He was for them Italy's first modern patriot. Curiously, both Hegel and Marx were among the famous political thinkers who sympathized with Machiavelli. Hegel, who had experienced Germany's humiliation after the battle of Jena in 1806, as well as Napoleon's policies in the German lands, considered Machiavelli a dignified patriot who was the first to have grasped the dangers posed by French imperialism to other nations. While Marx openly postulated that Machiavelli was the first modern political thinker to have demystified politics and power.

Politics cannot exist without that which creates the miracle of sociability, the associative link among people. It cannot exist without norms, beliefs, and values. Technique and mechanics shortly become caricatures whenever they are torn from goals and meaning. Machiavelli never asserted that politics is required to be amoral. He only demonstrated that these spheres have an autonomy and logic of their own, while at the same time they are possible without each other. Yet many writers and commentators were tempted to accuse Machiavelli of almost every dubious tendency of modern politics. Machiavelli was deplored by the great English poets and dramatists of the Elizabethan epoch. He had no shortage of admirers, starting with Johann Gottfried von Herder, Johann Gottlieb Fichte, Hegel, Marx, and ending with the Carbonari and the heroes of the *Risorgimento*, the war for Italian unification.

And so I am re-reading *The Prince*, meant for a legitimate monarch or a despot who has usurped the reigns of state power, at the same time as I read

*The Modern Who Believed that He Was the Ancient:*
*Niccolò Machiavelli in European Thought and Political Imagination* 55

Machiavelli's other work geared for republicans and citizens, especially that work which is far more serious from a theoretical viewpoint, *The Discourses on Livy*. As I read, I see that such a thinker could only have arisen in a country where the Church had far greater political power than any other European country. From this arose his antagonism to the politics of Pope Alexander VI, and his admiration for the activities of the "Duca Valentino" (Duke Valentine), Cesare Borgia, who united Romagna and centralized political power and the state in a formerly fragmented and weak Italy.

As he observed the unfolding of events in Italy, Machiavelli rejected the sacred origins of the state and the idea of the divine right of kings. Ernst Cassirer has remarked accurately that in an era that was so rife with blood and license, only people who were completely disconnected and without any reference point from reality could have been capable of believing that the right to govern was something divinely bestowed (see Cassirer, 1974, 133–139). Machiavelli idealized the ancient pagan Roman Republic, believing firmly that paganism was far more effective than Christianity politically, created as it was for the salvation of the individual soul and not for the consolidation of a political nation and the creation of martial spirit and glory.

Europe, or, more precisely, conservative thinkers and writers, has never forgiven Machiavelli for his overt admiration for the pagan world, for his bravery and civic virtues, and, most importantly, for his disqualification of Christianity from politics and his desacralization of political power. Such an era offered only two paths: (1) that of Martin Luther and other religious reformers to rise up against the corrupt political power of the Pope, rife with plays for power, or (2) a radical criticism of Machiavelli's own era, holding it against the light of the wisdom and virtue of the Ancient World. The great majority of humanists chose the first path, choosing not *devotio moderna* and religious reform, but *studia humanitatis* and the rediscovery of the past as an alternative to the broken present. On this path, Machiavelli joined Thomas More, Erasmus of Rotterdam, and François Rabelais. Compared to these Renaissance thinkers, his contemporaries, Machiavelli's fate was unenviable. Probably no other Renaissance writer has been read letter-by-letter and word-for-word. All who grasp a modicum of the symbolic thinking of the Renaissance, its anti-genres, satires and parodies, its grotesque, its esotericism, and the carnival-like culture of its language and humor, agree that we cannot read More's *Utopia* and Erasmus's *Praise of Folly* letter-by-letter, since these works, just as Rabelais's *Gargantua and Pantagruel* (1532–1564), require especially complex hermeneutics.

Why, then, is Machiavelli, a contemporary of these writers and thinkers who made use of a multitude of devices and symbols of coded language, read letter-by-letter to this very day? Even the lion and fox metaphors are not as clear and simple as they may seem, as is often remarked by those who lack the erudition for a serious reading of Machiavelli.

Even more frequently, Machiavelli is treated unhistorically. Here I do not imply that all ideas need to be wrapped around their historical context and that everything should be explained in this manner. But if you do not pay heed to the situation of a person who threw out a challenge to the Medici family that ruled Florence for over three hundred years (barring a few interludes), that would mean you have not grasped the political life and logic of Florence during his era.

After all, Girolamo Savonarola, the Dominican monk who protested Alexander VI's immorality and cynicism, was killed before Machiavelli's very eyes in Florence's Piazza della Signoria. Piero Soderini, Florence's goodhearted Gonfaloniere, who did not heed Machiavelli's advice to never allow his enemies in place, but to kill them, deport them once and for all or repeatedly, or constantly spy upon their place of abode, was later toppled by the Medici and was forced to flee Florence.

This is the origin of Machiavelli's affixing to the roll call of people who are good, noble, but devoid of political instincts and power (*animo*, *virtù*, and Lady Fortune), the fragile and vulnerable who are poised to become easy plunder for villains. Does Machiavelli's antagonism to the powerful and unscrupulous Medici family really bear witness to his lack of principles and opportunism?

We cannot portray Machiavelli as an angel. He was an ambivalent and dangerous thinker who had lost faith in the instructive powers of politics and who openly professed politics alone as the mechanics of the state. He identified truth with successful practice. In Machiavelli's view, political practice is not constructed of norms and principles, but of its opposite, successful and historically tried-and-true experience. Efficacious truth (*verità effettuale*) is nothing other than successful practice, which is obliged to create a normative dimension in politics and become a recognized form of wisdom.

Machiavelli's roots in ancient historiography are deep and obvious. For Machiavelli, as for Plutarch before him, history and circumstance offer occasions (Fortune) for taking actions (*virtù*). The readiness to act is far more important than theoretical arguments or abstract truth. A profound internalization of politics that allows political problems to permeate your personality and become your existential concerns, suggests Machiavelli to have been close to what might be described as a political existentialism.

Yet we need to admit the breakthrough in the history of political thought, one far greater than the frank counsels offered to Lorenzo de' Medici, to whom *The Prince* is dedicated, which was shocking to Machiavelli's contemporaries. Machiavelli's modern ideas were exceptionally resonant during his era, and they were innovative and inspiring for nineteenth-century thinkers. In simple terms, successful and invincible beasts give rise to institutions and to political and ethical norms and codes of conduct. This was written more than three hundred years before Nietzsche! The idea that truth is accomplished practice that has been tested by history, rather than theorists, could have had impact on Marx.

And that is without considering Machiavelli's insight about religion, which, he says, is essential to a society from a practical viewpoint, as a force that mobilizes, conditions behavior, and provides a useful framework for society.

*The Modern Who Believed that He Was the Ancient:*
*Niccolò Machiavelli in European Thought and Political Imagination* 57

Religion is a social construct, without which any civilized or organized social existence would be impossible. After all, the people do not require complex instruction on faith or, worse, theological disputes. Practical truths help them orient themselves.

What could Voltaire have added to this?

### 3. The Footprints of Machiavelli's Thought in Stendhal

Another book that reveals much of the footprints of Machiavelli's thought in modern Europe is Stendhal's *Les chroniques italiennes* (*Three Italian Chronicles*, 1839) (see Stendhal, 1973; Stendhal, 1991). In one of his short novellas, "The Cenci," Stendhal expressed the idea that Don Juan is a *bona fide* Christian phenomenon if only because passion and pleasure are unable to go unmarked by sin and evil in Christian Europe. How many young and wealthy rakes, such as Tirso de Molina's Don Juan and, later, Molière's Don Juan, went completely unnoticed in ancient Athens and Rome? But in those societies, religion was a feast that encouraged people to enjoy life, which, as we know, was something to which Europe was later unable to reconcile itself.

Hence, a deep gulf between a pleasure and a religious sentiment in modern Europe. If you aim at something pleasant, sooner or later you will feel the touch of a sin, which inevitably makes the search for pleasure nothing short of a revolt against the rigid norms and conventions. Here is the best example of this encounter of pagan and Christian sensibilities deeply embedded in Don Juan and his modernized version, Marquis de Sade, although this example deals with a mundane episode: "It was in Italy and in the seventeenth century that a Princess said, as she sipped an ice with keen enjoyment on the evening of a hot day: 'What a pity, this is not a sin!'" (Stendhal, 1991, 7). In fact, this is the cultural code that deeply permeates European aristocracy: "Quel dommage que ce ne soit pas un péché!" (Stendhal, 1973, 52)

In this context, Callimaco from *Mandragola*, who openly celebrates passion and pleasure revealing Machiavelli's strikingly pagan and un-Christian attitude to love, appears to have been one of those young and wealthy rakes. The character who acts as if he were straight out of an ancient Roman comedy, Callimaco is depicted as a Florentine rake to allow Machiavelli to satirize the human nature and corrupt practices so manifest in his hometown.

According to Stendhal, passion is calamitous, while pleasure is sinful only where it is contrasted to religious sentiment, and the great European Renaissance, especially Italy, sought to reconcile these two sentiments. Stendhal noted that we are forever repeating that Christianity softens traditions and people's feelings. This may be true, but it gives rise to the question whether the ancient world would not have achieved this had it existed longer. According to Stendhal, *The Aeneid* is far gentler than *The Iliad*. Stendhal's insight into the civilizing process and the softening of manners as manifest in literature echoes Giambattista Vico's ideas.

This is how literature approaches a philosophical problem. Were the ideas expressed by Stendhal in this book pasted into works by Niccolò Machiavelli, Giambattista Vico, or David Hume, it would not bring them any shame. Stendhal's thoughts are not out of place in the works of philosophers who were his contemporaries. Stendhal, in this case, can be linked to the debate started by Machiavelli, and continued by Sir Francis Bacon, about what essential advantages modern Europe, with its scholarship and culture, had over the Ancient World.

Or, in the end, was modern Europe only a continuous distancing from the great classical period and its ideals? This is one of the major questions whose moral and theoretical tensions formed Europe's identity. We refer to this great theoretical encounter as the debate between the Ancients and the Moderns, the latter group being strongly associated with Sir Francis Bacon, and the former with Machiavelli.

Another novella by Stendhal, which addresses Machiavelli even more, is "Vanina Vanini." It is the story of a nineteenth-century Italian woman aristocrat, who falls in love with the nineteen-year old Carbonaro, Pietro Missirilli, who has escaped from prison, injured, and who has been given refuge in Vanina's father's home. Even though the story is set in 1832, allusions occur to the pre-Shakespearean early Renaissance novella about the beginnings of Romeo and Juliet's love. In Luigi da Porto's version of it, Juliet falls in love with Romeo dressed in women's clothing, or, at least, she cannot take her eyes off him. As we know, Shakespeare based his tragedy not on the version by Luigi da Porto, but the later one by Matteo Bandello.

In Stendhal's work, Vanina falls in love with the wounded pretty girl Clementina or is besotted with her beauty. She is revealed soon after as the wounded escaped Carbonaro Pietro. His innocent nineteen-year-old face, angelic eyes, and long hair allow him to disguise himself as a girl. A passionate romance ensues that sees the madly smitten Vanina reaching the painful realization that for her beloved the *venta* (a unit of the Carbonari) and the fight for Italian independence are more important than her.

After a period of abetting the Carbonari and using her wealth to obtain better ordnance, Vanina learns that Pietro and his unit are preparing an especially risky but clever conspiracy against the government. She betrays his comrades without naming Missirilli. All are arrested; Pietro comes under suspicion and, unable to bear the terrible sorrow and horror of having remained free, turns himself in to the authorities. In an attempt to rescue Pietro, Vanina goes to exceptional lengths. She agrees to marry a wealthy Roman aristocrat who is her devoted admirer and who has influential political ties.

Vanina manages to visit Pietro, but in prison he becomes an even more fervent patriot, while his love for Italy is accompanied by a strengthened religious sentiment with interludes of fatalism. After telling Missirilli that their love has no future and that he is first and foremost an Italian patriot whose life belongs to the homeland, Vanina admits that she has committed a terrible crime by betraying his unit. And because one of Missirilli's cohorts kills himself as he is being escorted to prison, she ends up with the weight of terrible crime on her conscience. The prison guard has to protect Vanina from Missirilli, who attempts to kill his disloyal lover with his chains. The story concludes with Missirilli still in jail, though Vanina manages to save his life, while Vanina marries the Duke Livio Savelli.

During one of his most passionate avowals of love, Missirilli cries out that he loves Vanina even more than life itself, that he would gladly go to America with her and be happy except for the woeful fact that Italy has yet to be liberated from the barbarian yoke. In another place, he vows to devote all of his energies to freeing Italy from the barbarians (Stendhal, 1991, 178). Quoting from the original, the punchline reads as follows: "Dès qu'il fut seul, il résolut de ne plus songer à la jeune Romaine qui l'avait oublié, et de consacrer toutes ses pensées au devoir de *délivrer l'Italie des barbares.*" (Stendhal, 1973, 323)

I found myself itching to find out who those barbarians were in the end. What does he mean by barbarians? As a child, I sensed instinctively that all those who sought to hinder noble Italy from achieving its freedom were the veritable barbarians. Was it Napoleon and the France of his era mentioned in the novella? The Austrians? Those Italians who collaborated with foreign powers, such as the Papal State and its carabinieri? Who, really?

Missirilli, when referring to the barbarian yoke, repeats Petrarch's words about the liberation of Italy from barbarians (*liberar l'Italia de' barbari*) uttered in 1350. Machiavelli was to repeat them at the end of *The Prince*, where he exhorted Lorenzo de' Medici to resolutely unite Italy and liberate it from the barbarian yoke (the French). These words were also repeated by Pope Julius II and eventually, long before George Gordon, Lord Byron, by the eighteenth-century Italian poet and dramatist Count Vittorio Alfieri, who deplored tyranny even more than Lord Byron (see ibid.). Count Alfieri called Machiavelli the "divine Machiavelli," *divino Machiavelli.*

Remarkably, Stendhal, a French writer, develops this theme and allows us to retrace Machiavelli's thought and sentiment back to the eighteenth and nineteenth centuries. This may strike you as incredible, until you have read Stendhal's novella, "The Duchess of Palliano," in which the prologue discusses the loss of Italian passion, its disappearance in the eighteenth century when, to their great loss, the Italian aristocracy imitated the cold and wholly indifferent upper classes of France and England. France's calamitous influence consisted in its demonstration of indifference toward everything and everyone and its studied masking of emotions, while England's disastrous influence was a stilted and all-effacing politeness to which one could add the affected boredom of its dandyism and the perfunctory stance toward everyone and anything.

Stendhal, in this superb study of mentalities and the history of customs, demonstrates the manner by which passion vanishes through the imitation of alien modes of aristocratic behavior. It was precisely his desire to discover

Italian passion that encouraged Stendhal to study and recount the chronicles of Renaissance Italy. Should we be surprised by this? Italian history, after all, rife as it was with passion, betrayal, and suffering, provided Shakespeare with much inspiration.

Stendhal wrote that fifteenth-century Paris, compared to the life of Italy's cities, was a city of admirable and pleasant barbarians. In the France of the time, women idolized only military leaders who were slated to be forgotten. Meanwhile, in Renaissance Italy a man who knew ancient Greek could be admired as much as any warrior. This happened in Italy, thanks to its passion and not the gallantry that stifles it (see Stendhal, 2010, 144–147). This is one more interpretive master stroke by Stendhal.

So, it is Stendhal who emerges as the discoverer of Renaissance Italy in Europe, where no one any longer believes in anything aside from power and prestige. Just as he emerges as the investigator of freedom, honor, and passion, disclosing their fate in periods where the dividing point between civilization and barbarity was quite unclear. As it is in our day.

### 4. Machiavelli's Challenge and Legacy

Florence, immoral and depraved as it was, did not need brutal military power to subjugate it. Mothers drove their daughters to sell their bodies for money. The same drive was conducted by men of the cloth with money, propelling into sin women who had come for confession. Its own decline and immorality posed a greater threat to Florence than any powerful and centralized state such as France and Italy. An amoral or immoral society cannot in principle be patriotic or self-conscious.

Not even weapons were required to conquer Florence. Florence could be defeated by allowing it to finally degenerate and drown in its internal turmoil and struggles over wealth, power, and prestige. Moral decrepitude inevitably ends in political collapse and the loss of liberty. Machiavelli, to whom all manner of sins are imputed, understood this better than any other political thinker.

In his view, Florence allowed itself to degenerate during the fifteenth century. Not only Italy's fragmentation and the terrible battles between the city-states, but also the absence of a dependable social and moral order, along with utter moral decrepitude, allowed any organized and centralized power to conquer Florence at will.

And this situation provides a thematic and problematic bridge to Machiavelli's *Prince*. Only a sovereign who had a perfect grasp of the technology of power and statecraft could have survived in a realm rife with such corruption and assassins-for-hire. Such a sovereign's goal would not be the power for its own sake, but, instead, the re-establishment of the law and order of the Roman Republic. In the end, Machiavelli was a Renaissance humanist and a passionate Florentine patriot who grasped the full extent of the decline of his native city and the emerging political dangers to which this gave rise.

## The Modern Who Believed that He Was the Ancient: Niccolò Machiavelli in European Thought and Political Imagination

The last thing I want to do is justify and bow to Machiavelli. All I hope to achieve is to interpret and understand him against the historical and political backdrop. Two Florentines of that era took notice of Florence's decline and of the immorality that was destroying it: Machiavelli and the Dominican friar, Girolamo Savonarola. Savonarola ruled Florence briefly after the toppling of the Medicis, gave fiery sermons, burned books and pictures publicly, destroyed "pagan" objects of art, and sought the creation of a Christian religious republic in Florence.

Even a war against immorality can transform into a hell for those caught in the wrong place or innocent bystanders, which is why what Savonarola's battle with the Renaissance might have led to remains unclear, since Pope Alexander VI put it down brutally. Suffice to recall that the Florentine painter Sandro Botticelli was forced by Savonarola to burn his paintings in public. Savonarola was accused of heresy and burned at the stake. Machiavelli witnessed and recorded his execution.

In this case, I am concerned by the fact that Savonarola believed that the active involvement of the Church in politics could vanquish society's moral decline. Machiavelli rejected this route and placed his faith in a brutal albeit civilized and secular political power that sought to revive the laws and institutions of the Roman Republic. How else could he influence the people that he portrayed in *Mandragola*? (See Machiavelli, 1980)

From this does not follow that all people are scoundrels. Those who portray society as a collection of cretins or a rogues' gallery have concealed, or open, tendencies toward brutal politics. From this viewpoint, Machiavelli went too far. In his comedy, Machiavelli introduces the character Ligurio as a parasite. A parasite, as a class or a social mask, was an impossible phenomenon in the New Era, if only because slavery no longer existed. The Parasite is a character in Plautus's comedy, *Miles Gloriosus*, who sponges off of wealthy and free people, a toady who entertains them with gossip, rumor, and jokes. Such freeloaders and hangers-on, stuck midway between slave and freeman, who almost belonged to a separate social class, were referred to by the ancient Greeks as sycophants.

Machiavelli, whom we can consider as having been the first representative of empirical political scholarship in Europe, as a prototype of a political sociologist, and perhaps even as the father of these disciplines, including the foundations he laid for political anthropology and political psychology, by means of the behavior of the actors on his political stage, and analytical model of their tendencies and customs, lays bare an anatomy of human corruption and venality. As someone who treated conspiracies seriously, and who studied them and held them to be inexorable parts of any political machine, Machiavelli raised these to the rank of objects for political analysis and broke ground for later pamphleteers to portray himself as a specialist concerning conspiracy.

In 1864, the French lawyer Maurice Joly (1829–1878) wrote a pamphlet, *Dialogue aux Enfers entre Montesquieu et Machiavel* (*The Dialogue in Hell between Montesquieu and Machiavelli*), which was a landmark pamphlet severely criticizing the despotism and political cynicism of Napoleon III. A brilliant stylist and a thoughtful political analyst, Joly composed his pamphlet in the form of a dialogue between Charles de Secondat, Baron de la Brède et de Montesquieu, and Machiavelli.

Whereas Montesquieu champions the values of liberalism and denounces immoral politics, suggesting that despotism has always been immoral, Machiavelli represents Napoleon III, solemnly and cynically pronouncing that politics has never had anything to do with morality. Joly's *Dialogue aux Enfers* was published after the appearance of Eugène Sue's novels on the Jesuit plot. What Sue described as the Jesuit plot, Joly attributed to Napoleon III: the rise of reaction and religious bigotry, shameless political manipulations, and cynical misuse of democratic institutions for the sake of tyranny.

Maurice Joly was an elegant writer and an original thinker, and he deserved a better fate than what awaited him. The political persecution and imprisonment he underwent, and even his suicide in 1878, were not the worst part of his destiny. The worst, that concerned his essay, was still to come. As we now know, Tsarist Russia's political police, *Okhrana*, forged the notorious *Protocols of the Elders of Zion* (forged between 1897 and 1898, and published in 1917) using Joly's book as a model. (see Donskis, 2003, 19–79)

Joly's concern with Machiavelli as representing modern immoral politics was by no means accidental. Machiavelli was surely the most explicit advocate and instructor of what we could well describe as the mechanics of government (see Copleston, 1963, 128–134). Machiavelli was immediately concerned with political mechanics and with the contemporary Italian scene, far more than with abstract political theory.

Although Harvey C. Mansfield suggested that Machiavelli's notion of conspiracies was a logical continuation of his concepts of *animo*, the spirit of self-defense, and *virtù*. According to Mansfield, *virtù*, in Machiavelli's philosophy, is not just another word for manliness, valor, and prowess, as many political theorists suggest. "Machiavelli's virtue is not ancient or Roman manliness" (Mansfield, 1998, 36). Yet it does not mean virtue in the classical sense. Machiavelli stood in sharp contrast to his predecessors, such classical political thinkers as Plato and Aristotle, who, though interested in concrete and practical politics, never abandoned their moral and educational concerns (see Machiavelli, 1998, 218–235; Mansfield, 1998, 36–52).

Mansfield notes,

> For Machiavelli, virtue does not consist in having a virtuous character, as for Aristotle. Virtue is alert, on the make; it is not a habit. One must of course get used to the exacting requirements of loose morals and to some extent learn by doing or at least pretending; the main need, however, is not habituation but new and better opinions, or the replacement of inadequate by adequate presumptions. (Ibid., 45)

## The Modern Who Believed that He Was the Ancient: Niccolò Machiavelli in European Thought and Political Imagination

Machiavelli's major works, *The Prince* and *The Discourses on Livy*, rest on his assertion that historical development is conditioned entirely by the intentions and deeds of those who occupy the limelight on the political stage (see Machiavelli, 2003; Machiavelli, 1998). This assertion was at the core of modern conspiracy theories, which were all ultimately based on the idea of intentional action as the principal driving force behind the scenes of political life. What is the conspiracy theory of society, if not a theory of political mechanics and of the naked technology of power, a theory devoid of all religious, educational, and moral aspects of politics?

In a way, the modern conspiracy theory of society received its impetus from Machiavelli, who deprived his political theory of all indispensable emphases on religious and moral aspects of politics, and who was least concerned with the *ought to be* as superior and prior to the *is*. Whereas classical political theory rested on, and was derived from, moral theory, Machiavelli emancipated political theory from moral theory.

This is not to say that Machiavelli was not a humanist, though. I would argue that he was one and that his applied and practical political philosophy merely reflected the real politics of his time. Yet the fact is that Machiavelli provided a new and viable framework for the conspiracy theory of society. Hence, a profound immorality intrinsic in all modern conspiracy theories as a frame of reference and as a point of departure. As Frederick Copleston points out,

> [Machiavelli] ... over-estimated the part played in historical development by politics in a narrow sense; and he failed to discern the importance of other factors, religious and social. ... Machiavelli was clever and brilliant; but he can scarcely be called a profound political philosopher. ... He was thus immediately concerned with political mechanics; but his outlook implied a certain philosophy of history. It implied, for example, that there is repetition in history and that history is of such a nature that it affords a basis for induction. Machiavelli's method was not ... altogether new. Aristotle ... certainly based his political ideas on an examination of actual institutions and he considered not only the ways in which States are destroyed but also the virtues which the ruler should pretend to have if he is to be successful. ... But Aristotle was much more concerned than Machiavelli with abstract theory. He was also primarily interested in political organizations as the setting for moral and intellectual education, whereas Machiavelli was much more interested in the actual nature and course of concrete political life. (Copleston, 1963, 134)

Machiavelli's principle of *verità effettuale* deeply penetrates modern political thought, not to mention mundane political reasoning and practice-and-achievement-oriented discourse of political efficiency. He, who outlives his foes and adversaries, exists from the political point of view. Truth coincides with successful practice, which means that adopted and institutionalized practices are real and true. The crime becomes a necessary measure or even a painful sacrifice insofar as the major political ends are achieved: for instance, if the state is successfully centralized. Yet those who fail to centralize the state are severely judged by the generations to come as cruel and senseless rulers.

In Machiavelli's border-value perspective, a blunder or a mistake is therefore worse than a crime. Small wonder, then, that the words allegedly said either by Antoine Boulay de la Meurthe, deputy from Meurthe in the *Corps législatif*, or by Napoleon's chief of police, Joseph Fouché, on the execution of Louis Antoine de Bourbon, Duke of Enghien, sound as if they were straight from Machiavelli: "C'est pire qu'un crime, c'est une faute" ("It is worse than a crime; it is a blunder"). This statement is sometimes attributed to the French diplomat Charles Maurice de Talleyrand-Périgord, the quote being given as "It is worse than a crime; it is a mistake." Therefore, a crime ceases to be a crime insofar as it serves a proper program or agenda or insofar as it brings the outcome that may become a blueprint for a viable social and moral order. A crime can be translated into virtue or at least a heroic deed, but a mistake cannot.

The difference between the national hero and the criminal is much in tune with this kind of reasoning: a successful and victorious criminal has every chance to pass for a hero, whereas a failed hero is portrayed by the winning power and the vocabulary it forges as a criminal. The dividing line remains quite thin, as if to say that it is all about who outlives who, and who imposes on who their practices, criteria, historical-political narrative, and moral vocabulary. Power is respected, whilst failures are despised. Whether we like it or not, this logic is deeply embedded in modern political thought.

Even at the beginning of the twenty-first century, we are likely to live in the world where successful exercise of power, be it plausible violence or good economic performance, increasingly becomes a license to abandon individual freedom, civil liberties, and human rights.

The same is true of uprisings vis-à-vis rebellions. As Blair Worden insightfully points out,

> Uprisings get called rebellions only when they fail. When they succeed, we subconsciously confer legitimacy on them and illegitimacy on the rulers they topple. Thus we do not think of Henry VII, who initiated the Tudor dynasty by overthrowing Richard III at Bosworth in 1485, as a rebel, as we would do if he had lost the battle. By the same token we do not apply the term "rebellion" to the uprising by Mary Tudor in 1553 ... that disproves the rule of the impotence of sixteenth-century insurrections. (Worden, 2010, 46)

Since *Quattrocento* Florence was a city of Neo-Platonists, that Aristotle's *Politics* was considered by Machiavelli a serious criterion in constructing a theory of political action and its underlying intentions is unlikely. That Machiavelli even constructed a theory in the classical sense is doubtful, for he made a collection of sketches and insights which had valuable theoretical implications for

## The Modern Who Believed that He Was the Ancient: Niccolò Machiavelli in European Thought and Political Imagination

modern political theory. Yet Machiavelli was a representative of the early historicism who believed firmly in the truth lurking within history. This is not the speculative truth discovered by the mind, but time-tested and efficacious practice. Practical wisdom and the power that crowns it bestow moral legitimacy.

Nonetheless, Machiavelli, as did later Francis Bacon, Giambattista Vico, and David Hume, believed that the truths he discovered do not belong to any single historical period, and are universal. Even if *The Prince* is considered a political document intended first and foremost for all Florence and for the Medicis, it is based on many centuries of confirmed truths about human nature. This is why there is no merit in limiting Machiavelli's analysis of immorality and corruption to his era alone. He addresses all of humanity from a historical perspective.

This supports the claim that Machiavelli was one of the first modern historical pessimists. His belief that the Christian world had lost authentic creative political powers reveals much about Machiavelli the admirer of the Ancient World. The Modern, though inclined to think of himself as the Ancient in the modern times, Machiavelli passionately defends that world against the follies of the modern world and its deviations from the ancient canon. Most importantly, he achieved a revolution in politics defending a kind of border-value morality, the priority of successful practice over detached principles, and other phenomena that we associate with modernity. Mansfield suggests that

> ... we are also uneasily aware that Machiavelli was, to say the least, present at the origin of a revolution in morality, which can be defined loosely in our terms as a change from virtue protected by religion to self-interest justified by secularism. The revolution is known to us, again using our word, as "modernity." (Ibid., 7–8)

Machiavelli appears to have been a modern revolutionary and a modern moral and political instrumentalist armed with the universal wisdom of Florentine humanism. This strange fusion gives rise to what we can term the great riddle of Machiavelli.

# WORKS CITED

Berlin, Isaiah. "The Originality of Machiavelli," Isaiah Berlin, *Against the Current: Essays in the History of Ideas*. London: Hogarth Press, 1979, pp. 25–79.
Cassirer, Ernst. *The Myth of the State*. London & New Haven, Conn.: Yale University Press, 1974.
Copleston, Frederick. *A History of Philosophy*. Vol. 3: *Late Mediaeval and Renaissance Philosophy*. Part II: *The Revival of Platonism to Suárez*. Garden City, N. Y.: Image Books, 1963.
Donskis, Leonidas. *Forms of Hatred: The Troubled Imagination in Modern Philosophy and Literature*. Amsterdam & New York: Rodopi, 2003.
Machiavelli, Niccolò. *Discourses on Livy* (1531). Chicago & London: University of Chicago Press, 1998.
———. *Mandragola* (1524). Indianapolis, Ind.: Bobbs-Merrill Educational Publishing, 1980.
———. *The Prince* (1532). Boston, Mass.: Dante University Press, 2003.
Mansfield, Harvey C. *Machiavelli's Virtue*. Chicago & London: University of Chicago Press, 1996.
Shakespeare, William. *The Tragedy of Romeo and Juliet* (1597). New York: Washington Square Press, 1992.
Stendhal. *The Abbess of Castro and Other Shorter Novels*. Gloucester, Gloucestershire, England: Dodo Press, 2010.
———. *Chroniques italiennes*. Paris: Gallimard: 1973.
———. *Three Italian Chronicles*. New York: New Directions, 1991.
White, Michael. *Machiavelli: A Man Misunderstood*. London: Abacus, 2005.
Worden, Blair. "The Fires of the Rebel Queen," in *The New York Review of Books*, Vol. LVII, No. 7, April 29 – May 12, 2010, pp. 46–50.

Five

# MACHIAVELLI AND THE THEORY OF EXEMPLARY CONSTITUTIONS

Cătălin Avramescu

**Abstract**

The purpose of my essay is to show that Venice and the Venetian government are central to Machiavelli's system of ideas. More importantly, the rise of the "new prince" is connected to the perspective of the downfall of Venice. Machiavelli's design is a complex plan to counter Venetian supremacy not just in the realm of experience, but primarily of Venice as an eminent model of a body-politic. The result is an analysis of the political regimes of Venice and of Florence in the context of a history of their origin, rise and expansion. Starting with the Discorsi, Machiavelli advances a complex theory of what I call "exemplary regimes." Here, he establishes two conceptual and historical threads. On the one hand, that of Venice, which is seen as the continuation of the Spartan constitutional tradition. On the other, that of Florence, which is connected with the constitutional tradition of Rome. This, above all other constitution, is "perfect" and a functional example of a "mixed" constitution. Florence is the modern, supreme, reiteration of it. Venice, in contrast, is declared responsible for the presence of the French in the Italian peninsula and the defects of its constitution revealed. According to Machiavelli, two models are all there is: "For I do not believe one can find a mode between one and the other." And his choice is clear: "I believe that it is necessary to follow the Roman order and not that of the other republics."

What may be the reasons, then, for Machiavelli to analyse, unfavourably, Venice? One answer may be, as recent scholarly literature demonstrates, the perception in Florence of certain political reforms, notably those of Savonarola, which were considered to have been inspired by example of the Venetian oligarchy. I think an alternative explanation is to consider elements of what was called the "myth of Venice" as predating the defeat of the Serenissima at the hands of the armies of the League of Cambrai at Agnadello, in 1509. There was, in fact, a tradition established by the first chronicle of Venice, of John the Deacon, which maintained the republic was a most "excellent" city. Ironically, it was this myth to found its way into Northern Europe and leave its mark on the development of political thought, the influence of Machiavelli's Prince and Discorsi notwithstanding.

"I shall set aside any discussion of republics, because I treated them elsewhere at length. I shall consider only the principality... and I shall discuss how these principalities can be governed and maintained,"[1] declares Machiavelli in the beginning of the second chapter of *The Prince*. He wouldn't be true to the spirit of Machiavellianism if this wasn't some sort of misleading statement. In a letter to Guicciardini, he admits that "for a long time I have not said what I believed, nor do I ever believe what I say, and if indeed sometimes I happen to tell the truth, I hide it among so many lies that it is hard to find." Of course Machiavelli discusses aspects of republican rule in *De principatibus*. In chapter X, for instance, the "free cities of Germany" are hailed as an example of excellence in the military arts, one that the even the new prince should be wise to emulate. Yet most modern commentators have taken him to his word and focused on the character of *The Prince*.

The evidence, however, is patchy. Yes, Machiavelli dedicated *De principatibus* to a prince. The trouble is that it doesn't seem to be quite sure to whom. First to Giuliano de Medici, Duke of Nemours, and afterwards to Lorenzo de Medici, Duke of Urbino. We know Machiavelli must have changed the dedication between 1516 and 1519, after the death of Giuliano and before the death of Lorenzo. *The Prince* was therefore often read simply as a work born of a particular necessity, penned by a discontented Republican supporter eager to find a new patron. Why not rush it to publication in 1513, then, when it was written, between July and December? It is likely that Machiavelli anticipated, indeed, a Medici alliance between Giuliano and Pope Leo X and that this was a major reason for composing *The Prince*. Still, this does not explain the text at a deeper level. Machiavelli was very fond of his science of politics and he often formulates what he takes to be general truths, as opposed to statements of circumstance.

Moreover, if the intended reader is principally *The Prince*, why bother to draw attention to the discussion of republics "treated elsewhere," especially since there is no satisfactory proof that the *Discorsi* were already well under way to be written in 1513? And why challenge *The Prince* into believing the author has put aside a lengthy treatise on republics, especially since that may contrast with the "little gift" of *The Prince*? Another anomaly: in the same paragraph, Machiavelli claims he is set to analyse the governing and maintaining of principalities. If fact, much of what Machiavelli does is to discuss the establishing of a city or a principality.

My goal, then, is to approach Machiavelli's *Prince* from a different angle. What I wish to demonstrate is that republics are, indeed, essential for the argument of the book. In particular, I would like to show that Venice and the Venetian government are central to Machiavelli's system of ideas. There is another reason than the princely addressee which explains Machiavelli's reluctance to openly take on the question of the Venetian political experience. The rise of the "new prince" is connected to the downfall of Venice. His is a complex plan to counter Venetian supremacy not just in the realm of experience, but primarily of Venice as an eminent model of a body-politic.

One preliminary question to be considered is just to what genre of text *De principatibus* belongs to. It goes without saying that to a considerable extent that work is original and I will leave the topic of eventual influences on Machiavelli for a later consideration. The problem is that the more original a work is, the more is appears, both to the authors and to contemporary readers, as an attempt to make a point simply through straying from the accepted norms. It matters, then, to understand what sort of text Machiavelli should have produced, as compared to what was effectively written, so that we may be aware of a space of signification into which the Italian author deploys his argumentation.

The tradition establishing that *The Prince* is a book in the tradition of the "mirror of princes" (*speculum principis, speculum regalae*) is embedded in books such as *Machiavelli's Prince And Its Forerunners; The Prince As a Typical Book "De Regimine Principum"* of Alan H. Gilbert (1968). At the same time, there seems to be a general consensus in the scholarly literature that Machiavelli is departing drastically from the conventions of this genre, most emphatically in the critique of traditional Christian values.

I shall begin by suggesting an alternative theoretical lineage. In fact, though it appears to have been cast in the mould established by previous examples of the "mirrors of princes" literature (such as John of Salisbury's *Policraticus* or John Skelton's *Speculum principis*), *The Prince* does differ from it in a crucial respect: it does not seem to be a pedagogical treatise, intended for the use of an established prince. On the contrary, apart from the emphasis on the "new prince," Machiavelli's small treatise appears to be focused squarely on what we call today the comparative study of the body politic.

Not any study, though. In order to understand the purpose of the comparison, let us remember that a cornerstone of classical (that is, pre-modern) political theory is the discourse on the classification of political regimes. Perhaps the earliest reference to what became the standard tripartite classification is that in Herodotus (*Histories*, III 80–82). Briefly, the criterion used to distinguish among forms of government is the number of those who rule: one, few or many. Combined with a second criterion, that of the quality of the rule (good or bad), one obtains the familiar classification of political regimes (monarchy-tyranny, aristocracy-oligarchy, and democracy-anarchy). This is the scheme that was used, with some variations, from Plato and Aristotle to the late 18th century.

One important aspect of this classification needs not to be overlooked here. As implied by the existence of the second criterion, regimes are not born equal. Classical authors were keenly aware of this. They discussed the hierarchy of regimes (in order to distinguish the nature of the "happiest" form of government (typically, monarchy, especially in the Middle Ages and the Renaissance). The identity of this felicitous form of government was, nevertheless, not simply a theoretical, abstract, issue. As the Ancients were also aware, all regimes are caught in a cycle of decay (again, Plato's *Republic* is good example of a perception which was commonplace until the Renaissance; witness Le Roy's *De la vicissitude ou variété des choses en l'univers*, 1577). The well-known answer to this universal tendency, inherent to all created things, was to speculate on the possibility of a sort of mixture between what are otherwise the pure forms of government. The result is the famous theory of the "mixed regime," usually associated with Polybius, but shown recently to have been based rather on Aristotle and transmitted to the Moderns through the scholastic theologians and early humanists (Aquinas, Gilles of Rome, Peter of Auvergne, John of Paris and Ptolemy of Lucca to Nicole Oresme, Contarini, Savonarola and Bruni)[2].

What matters to our discussion is that identifying and describing this mixture was usually seen as a practical issue, not a theoretical one. The warning of Aristotle, who declared in his *Politics* (1290a) that there are as many forms of constitution as there are modes of arranging the public offices appears to have been heeded. Aristotle's position, in Books III and IV of the *Politics*, is that "simple" regimes are not, in fact, simple, *e. g.* the rule of the many where the majority is rich, like in a standard oligarchy. That is why we should not confuse the theoretical approach, closely related to the normal classification of regimes, with that on the "realistic" constitution. Let us consider this first species the discourse on the "ideal constitution" and the second, for lack of a better term, the discourse on the "exemplary constitution."

This latter genre is one with roots in Classical Antiquity. Writers like Xenophon and Isocrates were among the first to draw attention to the virtues of the Egyptian and Persian kingdoms. It was Aristotle, however, who discussed the merits of the constitutions of Sparta, Athens, Carthage or Crete, with the suggestion that some of these are to be regarded as stable and just. Perhaps the most influential such exemplary constitution was that of Rome, with Polybius as chief propagandist. Later, in the modern age, the English and the American constitutions will be inspired by the examples of republican and imperial Rome and will become, in their turn, sources of inspiration. In the late Enlightenment this pattern is clearly seen, as for instance in the praise of the English constitution by Voltaire or De Lolme.

The discussion on the exemplary constitutions squared nicely with the guidelines established by Aristotelian and Medieval theory of argumentation. The Latin *exemplum* is a widely-used term; it refers to the use of an image to make a point, to advance a claim. Often, this use is deployed in the context of a casuistic demonstration, which professes scepticism towards general rules and strives towards understanding the merits of each individual case. That the casuistic approach is not limited to the dissection of the moral dilemmas of the individuals and instead it is, at times, applied to the study of the body politic it is evident in the fusion between casuistic arguments and theoretical analysis in Hobbes's political treatises, especially the chapters on the forms of government such as monarchy.[3]

That Machiavelli elaborates a theory of the exemplary constitution would come as no surprise. Commentators have focused on two such constitutions exalted by the Italian thinker: Rome and Florence. The Tuscan republic is most famously depicted in *Istorie florentine* (1525) while Rome, especially republican Rome, is constantly referred to in *De principatibus* and, naturally, in *Discorsi*. My concern here is to show to what extent Venice is perceived as an exemplary constitution and to argue that the theory of the "new prince" is connected to this.

Before this, let us first dispel a historical misunderstanding. Machiavelli, in the final paragraphs of *The Prince*, formulates an exhortation to liberate Italy from the yoke of the "barbarians." He refers, certainly, to the Spanish, to the Swiss mercenaries and, above all, to the French. This does not mean, however, that his attitude towards France is altogether hostile. He does not oppose the quasi-republican prince of *De principatibus* to the French monarchy. In *Ritratto delle cose di Francia* (1510), written shortly before *The Prince*, as a good connoisseur of things French, he sketches a detailed portrait of France. This topic is again developed in the fourth chapter of *The Prince*, where he favourably compares France to Turkey. The clearest reference to France, however, is in chapter XIX. Here, France is a kingdom "well organized and well governed," a good example of political prudence, since the king has wisely delegated distasteful tasks to others, while keeping the pleasant burdens of government to himself.

It is, in fact, rather the Venetians who are responsible for the presence of the French in Italy. In the third chapter of *De principatibus* Machiavelli asserts dryly that "King Louis was installed in Italy because of the ambition of the Venetians, who wanted by his coming to gain for themselves half of Lombardy." He refrains from criticising the enterprise of the French king, as "he was forced to take whatever friendships he could," even though this resulted in the occupation of a third of Italy; Venetians, however, have proved to have acted "recklessly."

The same third chapter provides another insight in Machiavelli's outlook. Sure, the French king made all five mistakes Machiavelli showed a prince has to avoid making them, like not sending people to establish colonies and such. Still, even those five mistakes would not have proved to be his undoing, save for a sixth: "that of reducing the Venetians' power." In Machiavelli's analysis, Venice appears as necessary for a balance of power that would oppose it and France to the rest of Italy, a valance of power, needless to say, favourable to the French king, as the rest of the Italian states "would not have the nerve to provoke both of them."

Insttead, it is rather the *Serenissima* which is in the line of fire of Machiavelli. His hostility towards Venice shows transparently in his *Discorso o dialogo intorno alla noastra lingua*, written at an uncertain date. Enumerating the regions of Italy from the point of view of their linguistic identity, Machiavelli finds only five: Lombardy, Romagna, Tuscany, the states of the Church and, finally, Naples. The absence of Sicily is perhaps unimportant, while the absence of Venice is probably not a simple slip of the pen. According to Machiavelli, there is no language that Italy can rightfully call "common"; if there are elements of a common language, though, these are based on the writings in the "Florentine language." That the exclusion of the Venetian is intentional, we can sense from another outburst from the same discourse. Some, Machiavelli claims, are "ungrateful" towards their fatherland and consider its language to be on a par with "Milan, Venice, Romagna and all the blasphemies from Lombardy."

In the final chapter of *The Prince*, there is a similar partial approach. In her present condition, Italy is "more enslaved than the Hebrews, more servile than the Persians, more scattered than the Athenians," a diagnostic which emphatically excludes Venice. Though *Serenissima* was also in a difficult position after the defeat inflicted by the League of Cambrai, Machiavelli wishes for a man who might put an end "to the plundering of Lombardy, the ransoms in the Kingdom of Naples and in Tuscany." No sympathy for Venice here.

That Machiavelli nourishes a degree of political hostility towards Venice and its system of government must have had something to do with the perceived Venetian influence in the political thought of Savonarola, the radical reformer of Florence, who seemed to favour an arrangement reminiscent of the oligarchy of the Council of Ten. It would be a mistake, though, to reduce Machiavelli's position to that of a pamphleteer. His aim is more complex.

An indication of this is the fact that Machiavelli analyses the political regimes of Venice and Florence in the context of a history of their origin and rise. In *Istorie fiorentine*, Venice rose from the habitations of people who took refuge in a lagoon. Thus, Venice was safe while the rest of Italy lay in ruins. On the other hand, the origins of Florence are similar to those of Rome.

It is, however, in *Discorsi* that Machiavelli advances a complex theory on the exemplary regimes. Here, he differentiates between two political lineages. In the first chapter of this work, he reformulates the theory on the humble beginnings of Athens and Venice. These cities were founded in secluded places and inhabited by a sparse population. They were exposed to preciously few dangers, so that "any small beginning would have enabled them to come to the greatness they have."[4] There is no need, then, to display the martial virtues that enabled other cities, most notably Rome and Florence, the latter being a colony of Rome.

Rome, above all other constitution, is "perfect." The reason for this is that it managed to retain a "mixed" constitution.[5] They key to Rome being capable of retaining its liberty for so long is that it allowed a degree of tumult and enmity between the people and the nobles. In Rome, the guarding of liberty was entrusted to the people, in Sparta and in Venice it was in the nobles.[6]

Two things should be noted here. Firstly, the connection theorized by Machiavelli between Venice and the other prominent name in the theory of exemplary constitution, apart of Rome: Sparta. It was Sparta and not Athens that was referred to in awe, from Antiquity to the second part of the 18th century[7]. Secondly, that Venice, exactly like Sparta, is indeed a candidate to the status of exemplary constitution. "It is necessary to examine" – states Machiavelli – "which of these republics made the better choice." Surprisingly, he admits that "the liberty of Sparta and Venice had a longer life than that of Rome." Another passage is worth quoting at length to notice to what extent Machiavelli considers this opposition to have explanatory force:

In the end, he who subtly examines the whole will draw this conclusion from it: you are reasoning either about a republic that wishes to make an empire, such as Rome, or about one for whom it is enough to maintain itself. In the first case, it is necessary to do everything as did Rome; in the second, it can imitate Venice and Sparta.

This opposition between the ways of Sparta/Venice and those of Rome is even more sharply described in the next chapter. Sparta and Venice concentrate political power in a small group. "This mode was given it by chance more than by the prudence of him who gave them laws." Sparta and Venice appear, therefore, to be at a disadvantage compared to Rome, as their organization does not seem to allow, in Machiavelli's judgement, much room for an expansionist policy[8]: "expansion is poison for such republics." His conclusion is categorical: "I believe that it is necessary to follow the Roman order and not that of the other republics." The two models are all there is: "for I do not believe one can find a mode between one and the other."[9] What is certain is that among "modern republics," the Venetian is "excellent."[10]

Excellent it may be, but the Venetian constitution is hardly perfect. A defect is the great division between the lesser and the upper ranks. In Venice, "there is still the error that a citizen who has had a great rank is ashamed to accept a lesser one, and the city consents to his being able to keep his distance from it."[11] In a similar vein, the Great Council of Venice is criticised for being able to omit to appoint successors to vacant positions in the city and in the colonies, something that creates "a very great disorder."[12]

A rare parallel between Venice and Florence is indicated by Machiavelli in *Discorsi* III, 12. There is an essential difference between the neighbours of the two cities, as the Florentines face cities that were accustomed to live freely, whilst Venetians are surrounded by cities which are not that "obstinate" to defend themselves, though these are considerably powerful than those around Florence.

As for Florence itself, for Machiavelli the similarities with Rome do not amount to an identity, though. We know that for him the only nation still following the example of the Ancients is the Swiss. On the other hand, corruption is not necessarily a bad thing, from within his historical logic. A prince who wishes to introduce the "new modes" inspired by the example of imperialist Rome will be lucky to be entrusted a corrupt city, ripe for change. In Tuscany, where there are three republics confined in a small space – Florence, Lucca and Siena – conditions are such that a degree of equality necessary to a "civil life" could be introduced "by a prudent man having knowledge of the ancient civilizations." Here we understand that Machiavelli is not simply an apologist of existing Florentine arrangements, as he implies that his is a yet-untried enterprise. This is described by Machiavelli in terms that do not exclude history. It was necessary, for instance, that Rome was taken by the French, in order for it to be reborn, "to regain new life and new virtue."[13]

The downfall of Venice is attributed by Machiavelli to an erroneous reaction to a species of geographic determinism. We noticed that Venice was, from its founding, different from other cities in that it did not required the usual fortifications as it was not exposed to the same dangers, due to its location in a lagoon. In chapter XII of *The Prince*, Machiavelli claims that as long as Venice has pursued a course of maritime expansion, "they operated securely and gloriously"; whereas when it has ceased relying on her own troops and employed mercenaries for the push inland, they lost "what has cost them eight hundred years of exhausting effort to acquire."

There is also a lack of political acumen which has led to the downfall of Venice, as the city did not understand the implications of her relying on the power of the king of France (this, in turn, gave occasion to the rise of the temporal power of the Church and of Spain in Italy). It could be that the reference to the lion and to the fox, from chapter XVIII of *The Prince* could be a cryptic reference to Venice, represented by the lion of St. Mark. The source of it is in Cicero, yet Machiavelli twists here its meaning far from the original. The fox, cunningly, avoids traps while "those who play only the part of the lion do not understand matters."[14]

The reason of Venice's decay, in the end, relate to a miscalculation that is not circumstantial, but is determined by the nature of its body politic itself. As a maritime republic, she was not used to the intricacies of waging war on the mainland. Therefore the Venetians were reluctant to delegate the absolute authority over the army to an admiral, fearing usurpation. Slowly, they came to rely instead on foreign generals. Apparently, Machiavelli speculates, the Venetians did not understand that it was easier for an admiral to adapt to land warfare, than it is for a general to understand the art of naval warfare.

Venice has, therefore, in Machiavelli, a paradoxical status. On the one hand, it is the leading example of a modern exemplary constitution. On the other hand, though, it is the criticism of the Venetian constitution which contributes to the advancing of the theory of the "new modes" in politics and to the intuition that Florence, perhaps, will some day be able to fill that role. A final issue, then, has to be clarified: that of the reason which makes Venice such a prominent issue in Machiavelli's thought.

It has been suggested that Machiavelli's interest in Venetian affairs was sparked by the political events in the Italian peninsula. In 1508 the League of Cambrai was formed, pitting the French and the Spanish kings, the Pope, and a number of Italian states against Venice. Next year, the forces of the *Serenissima* were defeated in the battle of Agnadello. Divisions in the ranks of the victors, however, prevented them from exploiting their victory and for a while Venice remained safe. In 1513, moreover, due to the shifting alliances, the Venetians found themselves on the same side with the French. I do not exclude that the writing of *The Prince* is related to this precise aspect of the war. On the other hand, Florentine internal politics might also have had a role. The reforms of Savonarola were perceived by some in Florence to come perilously close to transforming the republic into a version of Venetian oligarchic government.

This might explain the interest Machiavelli took in the Venetians affairs and even in the Venetian government itself, but does not clarify fully why Machiavelli discusses Venice as a prominent example of constitution, as comparable to that of Rome.

It has been suggested by historians, most notable by William J. Bowsma[15] that the city was at the centre of what was often called the "myth of Venice." The problem with this interpretation is that, according again to Bowsma, the myth of Venice started to be constructed after the defeat of 1509, as a compensation for the losses suffered in the first part of the war. Moreover, the two main authors who propagated the image of a glorious Venice ruled by a form of government superior to all others, Gasparo Contarini (*De magistratibus et republica venetorum*, 1531) or Donato Giannotti (*Della repubblica de viniziani*, 1526), published their writings after Machiavelli.

It is not impossible that Machiavelli reacted to the very first signs of the cult for the Venetian government. I would suggest, nevertheless, a different approach. What Machiavelli had in mind is indeed the "myth of Venice." This myth, however, has not begun in after 1509. In fact, there is plenty of documentary evidence that it was around for century and that it was intentionally cultivated by the Venetian aristocracy[16].

The first chronicle of Venice, of John the Deacon, claims Venice is an "excellent province" and that the name of the city, derived from Greek, means "worthy of praise." Next generation of Venetian rules have started to claim a divinely-appointed role for the city. This is connected to the import of images and symbols from the Byzantine empire, of which Venice was for a long time a part (though only in name, at times). With the commercial expansion of the 13th century, the self-glorification of the city attained new heights. The arrival of the relics of St. Mark and the newly found emblem of the city, the winged lion holding a book are part of that process. A 13th century chronicle, that of Martino da Canal, claims that the "noble city" is the most beautiful in the world and that Mark's remains being brought to the city are connected with a prophetic dream of the Evangelist. In 1292, another chronicle, that of "Marco," claims the Venetians were originally Trojans.

The myth of Venice, in the 16th century, found its way northwards, when it entered the modern political imagination. It became popular especially in the 16th century, most notably in England. It is ironic that the English "Machiavellians," such as James Harrington, where in fact admirers of the Venetian system of government. Their theory rose to prominence so much that elements of the Venetian constitution entered the mainstream of political thought. Venice herself prospered for another two centuries, until its demise, at the hands of Napoleon, in 1797, after more than 1000 years of republican government.

In *Dell' arte della Guerra* (1521) Machiavelli claimed Venice had the opportunities to establish a "universal monarchy," if they only had known and understood the principles of politics. History proved the myth of Venice far more resilient than Machiavelli expected. Even prophets are mistaken, sometimes.

## NOTES

1. All quotes from *The Prince* are from the English translation of Peter Bondanella and Mark Musa (Oxford University Press, 1984)
2. See James M. Blythe, *Ideal Government and the Mixed Constitution in the Middle Ages* (Princeton University Press, 1992).
3. I discussed in detail this point in the introductory study ("*Un mic tratat despre păcat*"/A Small Treatise on Sin) to the Romanian translation of Hobbes's *Elements of Law*, where I showed, for instance, similarities between Hobbes's approach and the *Summa theological* of Aquinas.
4. Machiavelli, *Discorsi*, pag. 7. All references to this work are from the English translation of Harvey C. Mansfield and Nathan Tarcov (University of Chicago Press, 1996).
5. *Discorsi*, pag. 14.
6. *Discorsi*, pag. 17.
7. See Elizabeth Rawson, *The Spartan Tradition in European Thought* (Oxford, 1969).
8. For the importance of an expansionist agenda inspired by the Roman example, see Mark Hulliung, *Citizen Machiavelli* (Princeton University Press, 1984); for a variation of this argument, see Mikael Hörnqvist, *Machiavelli and Empire* (Cambridge University Press, 2004, who detects a modern, Florentine imperialist and republican ideology.
9. It is interesting to notice Machiavelli does not appear to be interested to include Israel in this list.
10. *Discorsi*, pag. 74.
11. *Discorsi*, pag. 77.
12. *Discorsi*, pag. 102.
13. *Discorsi*, pag. 209. The Phoenix is an alchemical symbol; for the influence of astrology and occultism in Machiavelli's thought, see Anthony J. Parel: *The Machiavellian Cosmos* (New Haven: Yale University Press, 1992).
14. Another cryptic reference to Venice could well be that in the final paragraph of chapter XIX of *The Prince*. This long chapter discussed the ways to avoid hatred and it refers to a long list of emperors. In the end, however, Machiavelli retains but two names. The new prince must, he states, "take from Severus those attributes which are necessary to found his state and from Marcus those which are suitable and glorious in order to conserve a state which is already established and stable."
15. See his *Venice and the Defense of Republican Liberty: Renaissance Values in the Age. of Counter-Reformation* (Berkeley and Los Angeles, 1969)
16. The following paragraph is based especially on Patricia Fortini Brown, *Venice and Antiquity: The Venetian Sense of the Past* (Yale University Press, 1996).

Part Two

# MACHIAVELLI AND CORE ISSUES IN MODERN POLITICAL PHILOSOPHY

Six

# VIRTUE IN HOBBES: SEEN FROM MACHIAVELLIAN POINT OF VIEW

Juhana Lemetti

**Abstract**

This paper discusses the notion of virtue in the civil philosophy of Hobbes. The view adopted is general and theoretical. The paper also takes up some recent interpretation of Hobbes's civil philosophy as a version of virtue ethics. In these terms the conclusion of the paper is negative. After giving some critical remarks, the paper suggests that instead of the traditional moral notion of virtue, Hobbes's discussion of virtues and their role in civil life is closer to Machiavelli's conception of *virtú*.

This paper discusses the notion of virtue in the civil philosophy of Thomas Hobbes (1588–1679) who is, with Niccolò Machiavelli (1469–1527), one of the two demons of modernity.[1] I will not cover the wide area of questions and problems related to this topic, but I will concentrate on the question: is virtue a meaningful way to conceptualise Hobbes's civil philosophy?

In order to answer, we need to understand the question, namely to have an initial idea of what virtue is.[2] The most obvious thing to say is that virtues are traits of (moral) character. They are something related to the kind of persons we are and, more precisely, how our characters reflect the interplay of our thoughts and actions. Correspondence between thought and action and the coherence of action are typical for a virtuous person. It is also, perhaps, safe to say that we tend to think that virtues have something to do with excellence, and more precisely, with laudability. A virtuous person and action have an element of (moral) excellence in the sense that to be virtuous is always something appreciated or valued by that person and others. Therefore, virtue also has a social component. As Hobbes writes in *Leviathan* (VIII, 32 and X, 42)[3]: "Vertue generally, in all sorts of subjects, is somewhat that is valued for eminence; and consisteth in comparison. For if all things were equally in all men, nothing would be prized," or more plainly, "The *Value*, or Worth of a man, is as of all other things, his Price; that is to say, so much as would be given for the use of his Power: and therefore is not absolute; but a thing dependant on the need and judgement of another."

In what follows, even though I utilise the introduced ideas, the interest is not in this sort of common wisdom, because I believe it to be misleading. Exactly why, I hope, becomes clear during the course of this paper. After reflecting on Hobbes's discussion of virtues and some of the related scholarship, I will express some worries about the whole setting. Then I shall introduce what I call the Machiavellian point of view, that is, how Machiavelli understood virtue. Lastly, I will evaluate whether Machiavellian's point of view could help to make sense of Hobbes's conception of virtue.

## Hobbes's Conception of Virtue

From *Leviathan* we learn three things about virtue.[4] First, Hobbes classifies virtues[5] which can be of two kinds: natural and artificial. Secondly, he speaks of virtues as certain kinds of traits of character. The last occurrence tells us that virtues were originally disposed to man by God, and that He did and does this by doctrine (that is, laws of nature), examples and occasions. Of these, the second one is central and it is extensively analysed in Hobbes's first published political treatise *On the Citizen*.[6] Here Hobbes writes:

> Reason teaches that *peace* is *good*; it follows by the same reason, that all the necessary means to peace are good also, and hence that *modesty, fairness, good faith, kindness*, and *mercy* (which we have proved above are necessary to peace), are *good manners* [*mores*] or habits, i. e., *virtues*. Hence by the very fact that *law* teaches the means to peace, it teaches *good manners* or virtues. (*On the Citizen* III. 31, 55. Cf. *The Elements of Law* XVII. 14, 98 and *Leviathan* XV, 79–80)[7]

The problem with virtues in general and of the preceding theories of virtues in particular, however, is that virtues are defined in many ways and seem to depend on circumstances and are, hence, easy to manipulate. This is worrisome for Hobbes and is clear in the following passage from *On the Citizen*:

> One must recognize that *good* and *evil* are names imposed on things to signify desire for or aversion for the things so named. Men's desires differ, as their temperaments, habits, and opinions differ; one may see this in the case of things perceived by the senses, by the taste, for instance, or by touch or smell, but it is much more so in everything to do with the ordinary actions of life; where what one man *praises*, i. e., calls *good*, the other *abuses* as *bad*; indeed the same man at different times *praises* or *blames* the same thing. This behaviour necessarily gives rise to discord and conflicts. […] The result has been that, though all agree in praise of the said virtues, they still disagree on their nature, that is, on what each one of them consists in. […] The same

action is approved by one party and called virtue, and criticized by others and construed as a vice. (*On the Citizen* III. 31–32, 55–56. Cf. *The Elements of Law* XVII. 14, 98–99)[8]

The more theoretical underlying reason is the Aristotelian doctrine of mean which fails to see that virtue is constituted by how actions contribute to the outmost aim of all humanity, i. e., peace. As Hobbes writes:

> Philosophers have heretofore found no remedy for this situation. For as they have not observed that the goodness of actions lies in their tendency to peace, their evil in their tendency to discord, they have constructed a *moral Philosophy* which is alien to the *moral law*, and inconsistent with itself. For they have {sic} taken this view that the nature of the *virtues* lies in a certain *mean* between two *extremes*, and vices in the *extremes* themselves, and this is patently false. (*On the Citizen* III. 32, 56)

Theoretically speaking, the mistake has been an un-scientific explanation of what virtue is about. It is about self-preservation which is the cornerstone of Hobbes's political theory and which determines his system of the laws of nature.

Practically speaking, virtues are integrated into Hobbes's theory of the absolute sovereignty. Hobbes justifies the absolute power of a sovereign by an argument which relies on the natural selfishness of human beings on one hand and the inevitable conflict that follows from the human capacity to manipulate words according to their own favour. The solution to this problem is familiar, but we find especially nice phrasing from *On the Citizen* (XVII. 12, 215), where Hobbes discusses one of the central virtues of humanity. Hobbes claims that because

> CHRIST gave no rule for this purpose {that is, how to decide what threatens the common good and social peace}; and indeed he did not come into this world to teach *logic*. The only thing left therefore is that the judges of such disputes be precisely those whom God had already instituted by nature, namely those appointed in each commonwealth by the sovereign.[...] For example, suppose a woman gives birth to a deformed figure, and the law forbids killing a human being, the question arises whether the new-born is a human being. The question then is, what is a human being? No one doubts that the commonwealth will decide – and without taking account of the Aristotelian definition, that a Man is a rational Animal.
>
> In brief, the sovereign decides the interpretation of the laws of nature and, actions according to this are virtuous, and the decisions of a sovereign are objective because they are based on the principle of (self-preservation).[9]

## Hobbes as Virtue Ethicist

As the above short discussion shows, there are both textual and philosophical reasons to believe that virtues have a role in Hobbes's civil philosophy. However, from this it does not necessarily follow that Hobbes is a virtue ethicists or a theorist of virtues.

There are a number of readings that consider the conception of virtue as central in Hobbes's moral or civil philosophy. Some of the readings seek to show that Hobbes's moral and/or civil philosophy, as a whole, makes most sense if seen as a version of virtue theory. For instance, Boonin-Vail (1994, 108) writes that "Hobbes is best understood as a sort of virtue ethicist" and Ewin (1991, 145) claims that Hobbes's "moral philosophy is a philosophy of virtues and vices, of qualities of character rather than of rules." The idea in both readings is essentially the same. Laws and the sanctions of the sovereign are not sufficient to achieve Hobbes's primary political goal which is peace and a commodious life. The problem thus far, these readings claim, has been that we have chosen the wrong product from the modern Wal-Mart of theoretical ethics. Instead of buying rule-egoism, contractarianism, deontological theory or good old utilitarianism, we should have picked up virtue ethics. Only this product is able to deal with the problem Hobbes's original text is supposed to pose and which is how genuine and stable co-operation is possible if we take such an individualistic theory of human motivation and rationality.[10] Theory of virtues is the best explanation of how we cope with each other and how the social cooperation in a pluralistic society is possible. In addition, the virtue theorist view explains why there is a relatively small amount of conflicts in a common-wealth. The key idea is that human beings, who tend to seek their private good, need to be habituated to overcome their natural selfishness and become decent subjects. As the most cogent argument in the field that is introduced by Skinner (1996, 11. Cf. Skinner 2002, Vol. 3, Chapter 4), echoes:

> Although Hobbes is often portrayed as the creator of an egoistic or a contractarian type of moral theory, I seek in chapters 8 and 9 to argue a strongly contracting case: that Hobbes is essentially a theorist of the virtues, whose civil science centres on the claim that the avoidance of the vices and the maintenance of social virtues are indispensable to the preservation of peace.

Skinner also gives a sober definition of what virtues are to Hobbes. They are "other qualities [than justice] indispensable to the maintenance of civic life' which however require a proper scientific analysis, after which they complete "a full-scale *scientia civilis*" (Skinner, 1996, 316). Later he distinguishes three central issues on Hobbes's conception of virtue: "the list of laws of nature is identical with the list of actions prescribed by reason for preserving our lives"; "those actions which contribute to preserving our lives by way of maintaining peace can in turn be described as instantiations of one or other of the leading social virtues of modesty, equity, trust, humanity, and mercy"; and, lastly and the most importantly that the mentioned qualities are virtues because they "conduce to the maintenance of peace." (Skinner, 1996, 323)

This reading appears to be congruent with the way virtues were discussed earlier. The problem is, as Skinner emphasises, that the very notion of virtue has been misunderstood. But why is this so important? When the concept of virtue is detached from this theoretical background, the problem of *paradiastole* is also solved. If an action does not – according to the sovereign – contribute to the maintenance of peace, it is not virtue, and if it does, it is. Hobbes gives a clear and indisputable criterion to determine what virtue is and what vice is, and therefore succeeds to give a true science of virtue and vice. And indeed, it appears that he is best read as a theorist of virtues. In the last section, I shall raise some doubts over this line of argument, and then I will end my discussion by explaining that Hobbes's conceptions of virtue may have a point of contact with Machiavelli.

## Virtue in Hobbes and the Machiavellian Point of View

My first worry relates to the notion of human nature. Despite the confusing idea of the Hobbesian man[11], Hobbes is an anti-essentialist. To him there is no idea of shared human nature, and he is quite strict in denying that there could be some sort of *summum bonum* or *telos* that constitutes human life (see above *Leviathan* XI, 48). Theory of virtue, instead, appears to entail not only an idea of a common shared good but above all, the uniformity of human nature. In light of this discrepancy in the basic view of human nature, it appears, at least problematic, to claim that Hobbes is seriously devoted to his virtue theory.

Secondly, and this is more or less subsequent to the first point, even Hobbes speaks of modesty, equity, humanity and so on, as well as this need to be read in context. Hobbes does not claim anywhere that people should aim for some specific moral standards. So in general, as in the case of the five basic social virtues, we need to remember that the laws of nature are not detailed moral prescriptions which tell people exactly what to do in order to be virtuous or vicious.

The third remark deals with a requirement of virtue ethics that was mentioned earlier, namely, the correspondence between thought and action. Hobbes's view of this correspondence is somewhat vague, as a central distinction of his civil philosophy demonstrates. Hobbes claims that the laws of nature (and thereby the five classical social virtues of modesty, equity, trust, humanity, and mercy) always oblige *in foro interno*, but only under certain conditions *in foro externo*. As Hobbes puts the issue in *On the Citizen* (III. 27, 54. Cf. *Elements of Law* XVII, 97; *Leviathan* XV, 79): "Hence the conclusion must be that a law of nature gives rise to an obligation in *the internal court* [*in Foro interno*] or *in conscience* always and everywhere, but *in the external court* [*in foro externo*] it gives rise to obligation only when it can be kept with safety".

This distinction is not compatible with the notion of virtue, at least, if we want to keep the idea that there needs to be correspondence between our thoughts and actions.

The fourth worry concerning the virtue ethicist's reading of Hobbes is based on the questioning of the premise that a peaceful and commodious living requires virtuous persons (or, to recall Skinner's claim that virtues are "indispensable to the preservation of peace") and offering an alternative explanation as to what creates the needed stability to the commonwealth. In normal conditions, the laws of nature work, not because people are virtuous, but because there are certain sub-state social structures like family.[12] Laws of nature are not manifestations of certain virtues, because laws of nature are not prescriptions, in a strong sense of the term, that are prevailing in virtue ethics. Instead, they are the principles of actions that rational human beings are recommended to follow, but which they do not necessarily follow, otherwise than, in their hearts. Through this clarification, the five social virtues in particular, and the five social virtues in general may be understood to describe certain traits of character that arise in certain conditions. What is, however, salient to notice is that these conditions that are certain social structures underlie traits of character and make them possible. In more theoretical terms, it is structure, not agency that explains the stability of commonwealths.

My last worry is, perhaps, also the most pressing one and relates to Hobbes's re-definition of the concept of virtue. The difference between him and most of his predecessors could be the following. Hobbes defines virtues in relation to an external standard, namely peace. It is exactly because of this radical shift, that it is very hard to see how these qualities could be traits of character or what is more, traits of moral character in the sense that these are understood in virtue ethics. They are external to a person, whereas virtue ethicists' views seem to suppose that virtuous traits of character are something that arises inside the person. And even Hobbes's idea that human beings are obliged to follow the laws of nature (including of being, say, modest, humane, and reliable) always *in foro interno* makes it possible to claim that he has a theory of character, but it needs to be admitted that this is somewhat of a thin conception of character.

Nevertheless, it is hard to deny that virtues do play a role in Hobbes. However, this role does not have so much to do with the more common or classical notion of virtue which emphasises morally laudable action. Therefore, I think that at least Boonin-Vail and Ewin are somewhat off the track with their interpretations of Hobbes as virtue ethicists. Skinner, who is more punctual, seems to offer a promising reading of the role of virtues in Hobbes, but he also pushes the idea of virtue too far by making them substantial traits of (moral) character that are necessary for the preservation of a commonwealth. Luckily we have Machiavelli.

Machiavelli turns the tables when it comes to virtue.[13] It is actually dubious whether Machiavelli's conception of *virtù* and the more general notion of virtue have much in common. Though there is both some historical (of this see below) and philosophical (the idea of excellency is the common denominator between the two) evidence that *virtú* and virtue have a point of contact, this question is largely skipped here. For the purposes of my suggestion, it is sufficient to point out that no matter how we understand the similarities between *virtú* and virtue; it is the differences between the two that are interesting. The second initial remark relates to the role of *virtú* in the different works of Machiavelli. Again there is some debate about the coherence of *virtú* in the works of Machiavelli, but here I take it as granted that his two principal works, *The Prince* and *Discourses*, are based on the same kind of or a similar enough of understanding of the concept.[14]

Machiavelli's discussion of *virtú* begins by reiterating the central ideas concerning virtue as these appeared in the Roman moralists (above all Cicero) and North-Italian humanists. For instance, he makes the distinction between the four cardinal virtues of prudence, temperance, fortitude, and justice and the special princely virtues of honesty, magnanimity, and liberality.[15] The difference, however, is the following. When the Roman moralists and their Renaissance followers emphasised that virtuous action pays back, that it is rational to be moral, Machiavelli ridiculed this assumption; "I shall set aside fantasies about rulers, then, and consider what happens in fact" (*The Prince* XV, 55). To believe that honesty is the best policy is naive. The natural selfishness of human beings is a more realistic starting point for politics.[16] As he writes in *The Prince* (Chapter XV, 54–55 and Chapter XVIII, 62):

> [H]ow men live is so different from how they should live that a ruler who does not do what is generally done, but persists in doing what ought to be done, will undermine his power than maintain it [...] a ruler who wishes to maintain his power must be prepared to act immorally when this becomes necessary.

And:

> And it must be understood that a ruler, and especially a new ruler, cannot always act in ways that are considered good because, in order to maintain his power, he is often forced to act treacherously, ruthlessly or inhumanely, and disregard the precepts of religion. Hence he must be prepared to vary his conduct as the winds of fortune and changing circumstances constrain him and, as I said before, not deviate from right conduct if possible, but be capable of entering upon the path of wrongdoing when this becomes necessary.[17]

To conclude, though I have not come across a detailed study of how Machiavelli influenced Hobbes, I suggest that Machiavelli's concept of *virtú* bears an interesting resemblance to Hobbes, at least in two respects.[18] First, we find a very Hobbesian tenet from Machiavelli, namely the central criterion of *virtú*, both in *The Prince* and in *Discourses*, as the willingness to do whatever is necessary for the preservation of one's government. Second, in *The Prince* – at least more openly than in *Discourses* – Machiavelli emphasises the idea that morality and rationality do not need to meet in a prince, and still we are talking about *virtú*. As Machiavelli, Hobbes seems to deny the relationship between morality and rationality as this was understood in the classical theory of virtue and, more broadly, in the classical political thought.[19] Acting virtuous for its own sake was an unrealistic assumption in the political climate of the late Renaissance and Early Modernity. If Hobbes was an ironical thinker, he couldn't contain himself merely to religion, but scorned some of the prevailing moral views and here, I believe, he learned much from Machiavelli.

# WORKS CITED

Aristotle, *The Complete Works of Aristotle*, 2 volumes, The revised Oxford translation, edited by Jonathan Barnes (Princeton University Press [UP], Princeton: NJ, 1984).

Baumgold, Deborah, *Hobbes's Political Theory* (Cambridge UP, Cambridge 1988).

Bock, Gisela et al. (eds.), *Machiavelli and republicanism* (Cambridge UP, Cambridge 1990).

Boonin-Vail, David, *Thomas Hobbes and the Science of Moral Virtue* (Cambridge UP, Cambridge 1992).

Ewin, R. E., *Virtues and Rights: The Moral Philosophy of Thomas Hobbes* (Westview, Boulder: CO, 1991).

Foisneau, Luc, "Leviathan's Theory of Justice," in Sorell and Foisneau (eds.) 2004, 105–122.

Hampton, Jean, *Hobbes and the Social Contract Tradition* (Cambridge UP, Cambridge 1986).

Hobbes, Thomas,

———. *The English Works of Thomas Hobbes*, 11 volumes, edited by Sir William Molesworth (Scientia, Aalen 1962).

———. *De Cive – The Latin Version*, edited by Howard Warrender (Oxford UP, 1983a).

———. *De Cive – The English Version*, edited by Howard Warrender (Oxford UP, 1983b).

———. *The Elements of Law*, edited by J.C.A. Gaskin (Oxford UP, Oxford 1992[1640]).

———. *Leviathan*, 2nd revised student edition, edited by Richard Tuck (Cambridge UP, Cambridge 1996).

———. *On the Citizen*, edited and translated by Richard Tuck and Michael Silverthorne (Cambridge UP, Cambridge 1998).

Hoekstra, Kinch, "The Savage, the Citizen, and the Foole – The Compulsion for Civil Society in the Philosophy of Thomas Hobbes" (Ph.D. thesis, Oxford University 1998).

Lemetti, Juhana, *Imagination and Diversity in the Philosophy of Hobbes* (Helsinki UP, Helsinki 2006).

Machiavelli, Niccolo, *The Prince*, edited by Quentin Skinner and Russell Price (Cambridge UP, Cambridge 1988).

Malcolm, Noel, *Aspects of Hobbes* (Oxford UP, Oxford 2002).

Pocock, J. G. A., *The Machiavellian Moment* (Princeton UP, Princeton: NJ, 1975).

Raab, Felix, *The English face of Machiavelli: A Changing Interpretation 1500–1700,* with a foreword by Hugh Trevor-Roper (University of Toronto Press, Toronto 1964).
Skinner, Quentin,
———. *Machiavelli* (Oxford UP, Oxford 1981).
———. "Introduction," in Machiavelli 1988, ix–xxiv.
———. *Reason and Rhetoric in the Philosophy of Hobbes* (Cambridge UP, Cambridge 1996).
———. *Liberty before Liberalism* (Cambridge UP, Cambridge 1998).
———. *Visions of Politics,* 3 volumes (Cambridge UP, Cambridge 2002).
Sorell, Tom,
———. *Hobbes* (Routledge & Kegan Paul, London 1986).
———. and Foisenau, Luc (eds.), *Leviathan After 350 Years* (Oxford UP, Oxford 2004)
Tuck, Richard,
———. *Hobbes* (Oxford UP, Oxford 1989).
———. *Philosophy and Government: 1572–1651* (Cambridge UP, Cambridge 1993).
Warrender, Howard, "Editor's Introduction', in Hobbes 1983b, 1–18.
Wolin, Sheldon, *Politics and Vision: Continuity and Innovation in Western Political Thought,* expanded edition (Princeton UP, Princeton: NJ 2004 [1960]).

## NOTES

1. Of Hobbes as a demon of modernity, see Tuck 1989, 100–103 and the works mentioned there.
2. In my opinion, the best introduction to the notion of virtue is still Aristotle's *Nicomachean Ethics*, Books II–IV.
3. References are given by chapters and page numbers, which follow the pagination of the Head edition of *Leviathan* and are indicated in the margins of the central modern editions of the work.
4. *Leviathan* VII; XV, 110; and XXXVI 228 ("For God disposeth men to piety, justice, mercy, truth, faith, and all manner of virtue, both moral, and intellectual, by doctrine, example, and by several occasions, natural, and ordinary"). An interesting analysis which is not discussed here is how Hobbes understood the depicting of virtues in literature, especially poetry, and what kind of virtues constitute a good author. Of these, see "Virtues concerning heroic poem", in *The English Works of Thomas Hobbes* [*EW*], Vol. X. For a discussion, see Lemetti 2006, chapter VI.
5. The distinction appears when Hobbes speaks of intellectual virtues, but I take it for granted that the distinction is applicable also to virtues in general and to moral virtues.
6. The work was published originally 1642 in Latin and is commonly known by its Latin title *De Cive*. The first English translation appeared 1650. Of the translation of *De Cive*, see War render 1983, 1–9 and Malcolm 2002, Chapter 8. The first political treatise Hobbes drafted was of course *The Elements of Law*, which was composed around 1640 but not published until 1650.
7. Two notes are appropriate here. First, by the deduction of modesty, fairness and so on Hobbes refers to the deduction of the ninth, the tenth, the second, the fourth, and the fifth law of nature from the fundamental law of nature. See, respectively, *On the Citizen* III.14, 50; III.15, 50; III.1, 43–44; III. 9, 48; and III.10, 48. Second,

Tuck's and Silverthorne's translation differs from common vocabulary. In the classical tradition the five social virtues were *modestia, æquitas, fides, humanitas,* and *misericordia,* which also appear in Hobbes's original Latin text (see *De Cive* III. 31, 120). The standard English translations are modesty, equity, trust, humanity, and mercy, which are also used in the 1650 translation and the translation that appears in *The English Works of Thomas Hobbes* as well as in research literature. Though Tuck's and Silverthorne's translation may catch some of the connotations these terms had to Hobbes, I have maintained the standard vocabulary.

8. In terms of the recent scholarship, they are vulnerable to a certain rhetoric re-description, that of, *paradiastole*. Of this see Skinner 1996, 317–318 and especially Skinner 2002, Vol. 3, Chapter 4.

9. Some clarifications are needed here. First, in Hobbes's text the term "self-preservation" is used when referred to individuals, whereas the term "preservation" is used when we speak of the aims of commonwealths, that is, collective agents. In an ideal case, self-preservation and preservation are one and the same, but in reality they are not. Second, much of the criticisms of Hobbes's theory of absolute sovereignty focus on the preference-order Hobbes seems to take, that is, that common preservation over-rules the private preservation. This makes Hobbes rather un-democratic thinker. In my opinion, this is a partly mistaken reading of Hobbes, for he holds (most clearly perhaps in *Leviathan*, Chapter XXI) that an individual always maintains his or her fundamental right to self-defence. Therefore, at least in the most obvious case, namely that when the sovereign threatens the life of an individual in the name of the common preservation of the commonwealth, the individual has the right to resist.

10. There are numerous studies on this problem. A comprehensive one is Hampton 1986.

11. As alluded to in footnote nine, this view is based on a superficial reading of Hobbes's psychology and a misunderstanding of the function of his concept of the state of nature in his political theory. For a balanced and critical view see Sorell 1986, Chapter VIII (which discusses extensively egoism in Hobbes) and Malcolm 2002, 30–31.

12. The best available study of the pre-political structures of sociability in Hobbes's civil philosophy is Hoekstra 1998. Another study worth of consulting is Baumgold 1988.

13. My reading of Machiavelli owns a great deal to the studies by Skinner. Of these see Skinner 1981, 1988, 2002, Vol. 2, Chapters 5 and 6. Of Machiavelli in general valuable are Pocock 1975 and Bock et al. (eds.) 1990. Of his influence to the English thinkers in the first half of 17th century consult Raab 1964 and, in some extent. Skinner 1998.

14. For similarities and differences between the two works and of the central notion of *virtú* see Skinner 1981, 50–57. In what follows I will concentrate on how *virtú* appears in *The Prince*. Any meticulous study of the role of *virtú* in *Discourses* and how it may connect to Hobbes's civil philosophy are beyond the scope of this paper.

15. See Chapters XV–XIX of *Prince*.

16. f the similarities between Machiavelli and Hobbes in this respect see Wolin 2004, 180–181.

17. Compare to Skinner (1988, xx): "To be a truly *virtuoso* prince is to be willing and able to do whatever is necessary for the preservation of one's government. So Machiavellian *virtù* consists in a willingness to follow the virtues when possible and an equal willingness to disregard them when necessary." Or in more positive terms, *virtù* is "the quality that enables us to endure our misfortune" (Skinner 1981, 53)
18. See however Tuck (1993, especially 279–283) which the most convincing study that at least the early Hobbes was influenced, if not directly, by Machiavelli, at least by the tradition Machiavelli greatly influenced to. For a rather contrasting view, that is, Hobbes as an anti-Machiavellian thinker, see Foisneau 2004, 117–120.
19. There is, however, a difference between the two thinkers that is worth mentioning. Even both show the appropriate suspiciousness of the classical idea that morality and politics smoothly agree, Hobbes seems to have a stronger commitment to certain core minimal morality that is based on the notion of preservation. For a more detailed study see Foisenau 2004.

# Seven

# RETHINKING MACHIAVELLI: REPUBLICANISM AND TOLERANCE

## Olli Loukola

**Abstract**

In this paper I will work with the concept of tolerance as it is attached to political institutions in the liberal and republican theories: what sorts of life styles, ends and goals are we to tolerate in our society? My starting point is, however, Machiavellis political theory, where the question would be, which are those ways of life that could not be tolerated, because they destroy *virtú*, the civic virtue, and thus disrupt society? Diversity, interdependence and political participation seem to be high up on the agenda, which Machiavelli and the contemporary republicanism share. The issues and concepts involved within my question-settings here range from individual liberty to the legitimacy of political institutions, from private pursuits to common goods, and from plurality to tolerance. There are the two central ideas involved in "tolerance." Firstly, what is it that makes some behaviour objectionable, and secondly, when is the society entitled to interfere with it? Republican theory shares with the liberal theory the emphasis on the worth of individuals, and parts company from the communitarian theory in the sense that common goods are politically realised goods, not pre-political shared values of the community. The central republican civic virtue is the willingness to deliberate; to reflect on opinions and communicate with others. Politics is thus not primarily a means for realising private interests, but a process of communication, through which common interests may be defined and realised. Yet social isolation and detachment from the political life is, and always has been, the greatest fear of the republican theory. These, I claim, are the kind of life styles, that the republican society can not tolerate. Such behaviour is objectionable and should be interfered with. It is the tasks of civic education, the deviance of which is not tolerated in the republican societies.

Like Isaiah Berlin says, "There is evidently something peculiarly disturbing about what Machiavelli said or implied, something that has caused profound and lasting uneasiness," while referring not only to the long lasting negative attitude towards Machiavelli, but also to the great number of articles and literature.[1] And he said this already 35 years ago.

The later interpretations of the 20th century – in particular those of Isaiah Berlin and Quentin Skinner – have changed the general focus from Machiavelli, the amoralist, to Machiavelli, the pluralist. This change is significant indeed, since, as we will see, it touches some of the key issues of our time, concerning pluralism and tolerance, individuals and communities, as well as institutional and state design.

Today, criticism against modernist and individualistic moral and political theorising has shifted from the traditional questions to more dispersed views of general human purposes and goals as well as the new characteristics that have arisen with modern and postmodern society. Also the recent developments of the world have forced us to re-evaluate the meaning and usefulness of the central terms and concepts traditionally used in our ethical and political discourses. The question I am starting from here is then, whether the Machiavellian vision of a good society, what politics is about – internally as well as internationally – how social dynamics operates, what social structure is like, and what the virtues of citizenship are, have something to offer to this world.

According to the traditional interpretation, it would be strange to find these sorts of concepts in Machiavelli, who in fact pictured the ways of the world through the metaphor of war,[2] in which only the toughest and the most scrupulous leaders – the ones most capable in the art of warfare[3] – survive. This is, what we must keep in mind, a conception that is strengthened by the fact, that the dominant and the traditional interpretation of Machiavelli is mainly based on *The Prince*, while Machiavelli reveals a completely different side of his thinking in *The Discourses*. It is the interpretations of this letter work that I will mainly deal with in this short essay.

All through Machiavelli's thinking there is a sort of a constant Janus-faced dualism, sometimes more and sometimes less hidden[4], which seems to cut through all his theory: there is two kinds of knowledge, the individuals' knowledge and gained through common pursuits; there are two kinds of lives, the private life and the public life; and two kinds of moralities, the Christian one and the pagan one, to mention a few. So what I am in fact saying here is that the main contribution of Machiavelli to contemporary political thought is his constant opposition to the monist tradition included in Western rationalism, but also his dualism or pluralism.

That Machiavelli in his political theory was also strongly influenced by the Roman republican thought is a well known fact. During the past 30 years or so, the emphasis in western political (analytic) philosophy has shifted from the liberal theory through communitarianism to republicanism: from the strong individualism of liberalism to the equally strong emphasis of the community and that of civic republicanism, the sort of a half-way theory of them both. Republicanism is a theory or an ideology that recognises the significance of private goals in society, yet acknowledges the not merely instrumental value of society for realising these goals, as did Machiavelli.[5] It is here, I think, that his importance for today is apparent. The common goals of society are not seen in this sense as universal, as if they were hardwired into human nature, or dictated by some cosmic force, but are freely negotiable and deliberated among the citizens in particular societies. This is the root of pluralism as well as republicanism, both ideologies the pioneer of which Machiavelli is often mentioned to be. The central question for both is, whether there are common goals, and if there are, what are they like, and how are we to determined them?

There are high hopes invested in contemporary republicanism as described by Iseult Honohan in her recent book *Civic Republicanism*. In the very first pages she writes that civic republicanism offers "an attractive way forward in a world of cultural diversity, global interdependence, inequality and environmental risk"; among the central questions here she itemises those of non-domination and political autonomy, participation and deliberation, and recognition and inclusion in a pluralist world.[6] These are surely no minor ambitions for any political theory or ideology to try to attain.

Diversity, interdependence and political participation then seem to be high up in the agenda of republicanism. Tolerance, for its part, is the concept through which I will examine these high ideals, and the question, whether Machiavelli's Janus-faced thinking, the tension between the non-scrupulous realist of *The Prince* and the benign republican of *The Discourses* is able to accommodate with them. There are naturally a great number of issues and concepts involved within such question-settings, but the ones I will be dealing with here are individual liberty to the legitimacy of political institutions, from private pursuits to common goods, from plurality to tolerance.

## Liberal Starting Points

My viewpoint here is that of a liberal theorist. Why? Because at face value liberalism seems to be the political theory, which takes both pluralism and tolerance seriously, due to its individualistic premises. The central purpose of the liberal theory is to safeguard individuals as well as groups in their endeavours from illegitimate inference of outsiders. As far as I see it, Machiavelli's ideas do not differ significantly from this. The liberal goal is to create them a secure sphere where they are free to lead their private lives as they see fit. This is also the main task of public institutions: they are to secure the freedom for everybody for their own way of life, to the extent it is possible.

But securing such a freedom is no easy task, as we are more willing the admit today than for instance 150 years ago. In the 19th century the burden of the white man was the civilisation of inferior races and less developed civilisations; and this attitude concerned not only distant countries and people of unusual skin colour, but also the less educated classes of his own country. This last issue was in fact central in the debates of the classical liberalism of the 19th century; who are those people who are educated, civilised and mature enough to be granted the liberty to conduct their own affairs? As has been noted a number of times, only white, male Westerners with the appropriate education, wealth and social status satisfied these criteria. Even though human equality has been part of the Western thinking for the past two thousand years, it has never really caught up with the real world events, not even today.

Individual liberty and freedom of thought were of course not an exclusive part of the classical liberalism but had emerged earlier as one of the central ideas of the enlightenment project. The purpose had been to emancipate people from the chains of blind faith, mystical beliefs, religious traditions, and oppressive governors – not a bad goal as such, by all means. The fact that the cure oftentimes turned out to be more deathly than the disease, was just as often belittled as part of the unfortunate, but necessary operating expenses. The white man's burden was, to put this monistic idea simply, that when you possess the truth and the knowledge of what the good of man is, this justifies preaching it to others and converting them – and I suppose, even makes it your moral duty. And there is obviously no place for tolerance here.

Liberalism is a strange and powerful theory in the sense that it is able to accommodate into its doctrines various ideological notions and conceptions. Even to an extent that I would hesitate to say that all the variations under the rubric of "liberalism" would have the same core values. Yet the concept of tolerance[7] has a very high ideological prestige in most liberal variations and practices. It is also immensely well immersed in our common consciousness as an individual virtue. Yet the liberal concept of tolerance involves great many problems.

There is a simple way of putting the central problem of tolerance. The origin of the use of the concept is in John Locke's "A Letter Concerning Tolerance" from 1690, "a plea for freedom of conscience and religious expression." Here Locke discusses in particular the dangers of using state power to fulfil religious goals. The goal of his paper was to outline the limits of social and political interference into the realm of personal belief. The crucial point is that tolerance here is a distinctively *political concept*, that is, an ideal aimed at limiting the power of public institutions, firstly and foremostly. That was the central task of Locke's political philosophy.

It is just as important to realise that the concept was certainly not universally or globally applicable for Locke. In his essay he in fact concentrated on tolerance between diverse Christian groups, like Catholics and Protestants; he for instance completely ruled out atheists and Jews of the group of those to be tolerated. This sounds like a rather limited concept of tolerance, and it does indeed have serious repercussions to the liberal theory. As John Grey puts it:

Liberal toleration began as a project of peaceful coexistence among communities of Christians whose rival claims to truth and political power had ended in war. The genealogy of toleration in the religious conflicts of early modern Europe makes it a poor guide to modus vivendi in the highly heterogeneous societies of late modem times.

Liberal toleration arose from the divisions of monocultural societies. In the conditions in which it arose, the liberal project of toleration made a signal contribution to human well-being. It allowed individuals and communities who did not share religious beliefs nevertheless to have some kind of life together. There are no imaginable circumstances in which human society can dispense with that project of toleration. Yet it has a limited relevance to the circumstances of the contemporary world. Liberal toleration presupposed a cultural consensus on values even as it allowed for differences in beliefs. It is an inadequate ideal in societies in which deep moral diversity has become an established fact of life.[8]

The idea of liberal virtue of tolerance has since Locke become a central part in the liberal theory, while these roots and deficiencies of the concept have been mostly forgotten. Moreover, toleration has become a common and a typically Western virtue, which many wish also to become a universal value. While in fact, if we are to believe Grey, multiculturalism, pluralism and confronting identities are tolerated merely to the extent that they do not threaten the common citizenship within the state and its foundational values. In this framework tolerance, according to Robert Paine, an anthropologist, signifies "an agenda of qualified sameness which is widely accepted as both sensible (not extreme) and, at the same time, "liberal" (civilised)." Unfortunately, as Paine continues, the underlying assumptions of universalism and common citizenship are rarely compatible with, and more often in contradiction to the assumptions of radically different communities, such as Paine's own example, the Australian Aboriginals.[9]

Thus we find severe limitations with the concept of toleration, especially when applied globally or universally. Is it the case that toleration is possible only when the groups tolerating each other are already, at the outset, similar enough in certain crucial respects, like Lockean people were? In that they all believe in Christian God? And just as importantly, when the destructive powers of all parties are equal enough, so that there is no gain in sight in warfare?

In fact it seems to me that today we are facing a situation where we are truly obliged to take all ways of life as equal This is a new situation in our world, and more importantly, it does not seem to solely based on the conviction that we are to be tolerant because of virtuous or moral reasons. In the light of the past events of this and the last century, we are simply forced to do that, because we cannot be sure any more, which part or group of the world possesses means of destruction, be they nuclear weapons, terrorists, globally spreading diseases, environmental hazards, or just simple masses of people. In some strange sense, we are getting equally powerful in this competition of existence and prosperity in this world of ours of diminishing resources. This seems to me to be a very Machiavellian setting indeed! And when we move newt to inspecting the way tolerance is in contemporary liberal theory delegated to political institutions, we surely have something more to learn from Machiavelli's political thought.

## From Tolerance to Neutrality

As I mentioned earlier, Locke started the political use of the concept of tolerance. The requirement of institutional impartiality or neutrality is the modern version of this concept of early liberalism.[10] This updated notion concerns the measures and actions, tasks and policies, licenses and duties of public institutions, not of individual citizens. When talking about tolerance, we are not now talking directly of whether I should tolerate you or that group of people to which you identify yourself. We are talking about political principles: what sorts of life styles and goals we are to tolerate in our society. This is where liberal theory moves those issues that should be tolerated into the category of "private" sphere, while the other issues, which are of greater importance to the society, are moved into the "political" sphere, to be decided together.

But the common goods are very scarce in the liberal society. It is the deep conviction of the liberal society that the goods and bads of the as well as ways of life are questions of private sphere, that is, individual discretion. And this is why – and I stress this point again – political institutions must remain neutral in the sense that they are not supposed the further any substantial goals; there are not really any substantial *common* goods in the liberal society. But the question then becomes, how do you know what a liberal society should tolerate? Surely not everything that the citizens do as "private" matters? The problem is that there are no directly applicable answers available to the question, what is of common importance and what is not to the liberal society. Except that of individual liberty, but again, it may be interpreted in a more inclusive or exclusive manner. As Berlin has put the issue as one concerning "negative" or "positive" liberty[11]. The question is then centrally of the role political institutions are to play in a society which consist of individuals furthering their private interests. From this starting points is possible to justify anything more extensive than neutral liberal institutions?

It is now time to move to Machiavelli's conception of political institutions and their roles. Just as in liberal theory it consists of individuals furthering their special interests. And Machiavelli also provides an account of liberty: why it is so important, how can it be sustained and what this sustenance requires. The following story is based on Quentin Skinner's well-known work[12] on Machiavelli.

**Skinner's Account of Machiavellian Liberty**

Contrary to *The Prince*, Machiavelli concentrates in *The Discourses* mainly in the republics, but with the more wider interest in mind, that is, what is the best way to govern cities in general. Why some cities "come to greatness" and others not? What is the basis of such "civic glory"?

By the use of his method, historical studies and political observations combined with the idea that "all cities and all peoples have the same desires and same traits," Machiavelli's purpose is to discover the cause for the greatness of ancient Rome. How could such greatness be reproduced in the governance of other cities? His answer was simple: "Experience shows that cities have never increased in dominion or riches except while they have been at liberty."

Like Skinner says, what Machiavelli had in mind with such a strong emphasis on liberty was, that any great city "must remain free from all forms of political servitude, whether imposed "internally" by the rule of a tyrant, or "externally" by an imperial power." And as Skinner continues, "[t]his in turn means that to say of a city that it possesses its liberty is equivalent to saying that it holds itself independent of any authority save that of the community itself"[13]. This means self-government, "a form of government based on the people"; and to Machiavelli this arrangement equates to living in liberty.

Machiavelli's open preference for republics is also to be found here, when he says at the beginning of the second Discourse that it is "not individual good, but common good" that "makes cities great," and that "without doubt this common good is thought important only in republics."[14]

After that Machiavelli – and Skinner – discuss, how liberty is to "be acquired, sustained and kept safe"? And here *virtú* and the goddess of Fortune enter the picture, as it does in *The Prince*. To start with, it is essential that the city is to have a free beginning, not to be dependent on anyone; with Fortune often at play. But the achievement of great things is never, as he says in *The Prince*, merely the outcome of good Fortune; it is always the product of Fortune combined with the indispensable quality of *virtú*. The civic glory of Rome was made possible by the fact that its citizens possessed so much *virtú*, that quality that enables us to endure our misfortunes with calmness and at the same time attract the favourable attention of Fortune. In *The Prince* Machiavelli associated *virtú* to political leaders and military commanders, but in *The Discourses* he says explicitly, that if a city is to attain greatness, it is essential that *the citizen body as a whole* should possess *virtú*.

Now *virtú* means the willingness to do whatever is necessary for the attainment of civic glory and greatness, even if the actions needed are as such considered evil. This of course is the familiar claim from *The Prince*, and the thing that so radically separated Machiavelli from the more classical writers of the same craft, such as Cicero, and earned Machiavelli his sinister later reputation. This trait, the willingness to place the good of the community above all private interests and all mundane conceptions of morality, is in *The Discourses* extended to ordinary citizens as well. And this is just as stringent demand for the citizens as it was for *The Prince*, that "there must be no consideration of just or unjust, of merciful or cruel, of praiseworthy or disgraceful; instead, setting aside every scruple, one must follow to the utmost any plan that will save her life and keep her liberty."[15] One is to put aside her own interest for the common good, the good of the common fatherland.

But how is one to keep up this quality of *virtú* in a community? Machiavelli talks about "first Fortune," the need for forefathers guiding the city to the right path from the very beginning, since no city – republic nor principality – could be built on *virtú* of the masses, "because their 'diverse opinions" will always prevent them from being 'suited to organise a government'." Therefore it is necessary to set up and organise the republic "alone," by one man only. But since men are mere mortals, the death of this one man would also deprive *virtú* of the community.[16] It is necessary to somehow make *virtú* lasting, to expand to the rest of the community as well.

We evidently cannot find *virtú* as naturally existing in citizens; Machiavelli was of the opinion that "most men 'are more prone to evil than to good', and in consequence they tend to ignore the interests of the community in order to act 'according to the wickedness of their spirits whenever they have a free scope." As a result, *virtú* will degenerate in one of two ways; either people lose their interest in politics altogether, and hence their concern for the common good. Or, more seriously still, they remain active in politics, but inflate it to the promotion of their personal interests or "factional loyalties" instead of that of the public interest.

So the vicious circle of the story is, that the preservation of liberty is necessary for the community's greatness, yet the growth of corruption is necessarily fatal to liberty, and when corruption takes fully over the citizen body, liberty too is lost. Now how can *virtú* be successfully implanted in the people who do not possess it naturally; how can they be prevented from sliding into corruption, and be coerced into keeping the goal of common good in their minds? The way this stage setting is built, it does indeed sound bad for any proponent of pluralism and tolerance.

If human nature is such, that *virtú* is not naturally engraved in it, it has to come from somewhere else than the minds and hearts of its citizens. The first suggestion Machiavelli presents is – quite consistently with his earlier views – an outstanding civic leader, a statesman, a general or a prince with enough personal character and *virtú* to influence lesser citizens. But as said earlier, this does not guarantee communal perseverance, which is Machiavelli's main interest – not to mention that the mere emergence of a virtuous leader in the first place is of course a matter of pure good Fortune.

This is where Machiavelli becomes most interesting for our present purposes. The key to sustaining *virtú* is to have the community organised so that it compels the citizens to acquire *virtú* and uphold their liberties – through institutions, political and constitutional arrangements and such. There are two methods in particular for this: the first is religious teaching and practices, which he sees to be of prime importance: "'one can have no better indication' of a country's corruption and ruin than 'to see divine worship little valued'."[17] Religious institutions can play the role of a virtuous leader; they can be used to induce citizens to prefer the good of their community to all other goods. It was, of course, not a new idea, that God-fearing communities will also profit in the achievement of civil glory, but again Machiavelli goes contrary to the dominant strain. For him, religion is a mere instrument for upholding the civic virtue; he had no interest in religious truth, but only in religion as "inspiring the people, in keeping men good, in making the wicked ashamed," and this is how he would grade the value of all existing religions. It is then no wonder that Christianity doesn't fare too well on this scale, with its otherworldly goals, its virtues of humbleness and humility and contempt for earthly human aspirations.[18]

The second, and more interesting method for sustaining *virtú* and achieving civic glory is the use of the coercive power of the law in order to force citizens to place the common good above their private pursuits. Good laws enable good education, which will in turn engrave *virtú* in the minds of the citizens. The heritage of the city is of prime importance here: if the city has had great lawgivers, such as Lycurgus of Sparta, then it has in its possession the rules, how to obtain civic greatness. This is something which the modern rulers can learn directly from the ancients, Machiavelli thought. He continues his study by investigating the three basic constitutional forms – monarch, aristocracy, and democracy – and finds them all corruptible. But mixed government combines and brings out the strong points of these three pure forms, as it did Machiavelli's prime example, the ancient republic of Rome. The republic enables the sustenance of *virtú* and upholding of liberty through the force of law.

## Monism, Dualism, or Pluralism?

It is here that Machiavelli takes up the issue that has made him one of the forefathers of pluralism and which has a direct bearing on the issue of tolerance. As I already mentioned, Machiavelli had a number of dualistic elements in his thinking. But does his dualism also lead lead to pluralism? Berlin seems to think so: "I regard Machiavelli as a dualist thinker. But once you have two equally valid possibilities you might have more. If there can be two answers, equally valid, to the same questions, there could be more."[19] And Berlin continues a bit later by stating that "[Machiavelli] is the first thinker who realized that there was more than one system of public values."[20]

In the history of philosophy there had been, before Machiavelli, a number of philosophers, who had theorised about the ultimate end of man, thinking that it is something universal, common to all men in all circumstances. In a similar manner, there had been those who had denied the existence of any perennial human ends. Plato was the best known example of the first kind and the sophists of the second. Yet Machiavelli seemed to have been the first to take seriously the idea that there are multitude of ultimate human ends existing in the society and concentrated in his thinking on how we should deal with them.

Machiavelli integrates this question into his story of the civic *virtú* and continues by talking of two opposed factions of the society, the normal people and the rich people. If constitution allows one or the other to take control, the republic will be corrupted. The party in power will rule according to its own interests and "the general good will become subordinated by factional loyalties, with the result that the *virtú* and in consequence the liberty of the republic will very soon be lost."[21]

The practical application arising from this insight was that the constitution should be devised in such a way that all factional loyalties and social forces existing in every society should remain in a carefully balanced equilibrium as well as involved in the business of government. Then they will all keep a close watch over others and jealously scrutinise each other for any attempts to reap power. This "resolution of the pressures thus engendered will mean that only those "laws and institutions" which are "conducive to public liberty" will actually be passed." Thus it is this tension between the various factions promoting their own interests that will in legislative matters result in public interest: "'all the laws made in favour of liberty' will 'result from their discord'," in a manner not unlike that of Adam Smith's invisible hand.

Like Skinner notes, this idea ran counter to the republican tradition of that time, tradition which used to outlaw all discord and factions as the most fatal threat to civic liberty[22]. This was one of the most cherished convictions of the Florentine humanism that Machiavelli attacked: that civil liberty requires one mind and the renunciation of all discords of society. Machiavelli writes that even though ancient Rome was so full of confusion, it is these discords that prevented prevailing of private interests and thus the first cause that kept Rome free.[23] Somehow these two aspects go hand in hand. As Machiavelli writes, private interests result in the end in the furtherance of public interest. Yet he also says that "one must follow to the utmost any plan that will save her life and keep her liberty," in a tone very similar to Hobbesian liberalism.

This is the topic relevant to tolerance arising from this Machiavellian account: how to manage between the variable and incompatible individual ends existing in every society and turn them into civic glory, the good of all, without unduly transgressing individual liberty. As usual, Machiavelli was probably never interested in whether there is some kind of truth involved in this competition of goals, whether one goal was somehow inherently more worthy than some other. The only criteria was, whether they further public interest and sustain or enhance liberty.

### Tolerance, Virtues, and Common Goods

In the flux of this discussion, my question has been, what tolerance would be in the republican theory. In other words, what are those issues, practices, traditions, or the ways of life, the various factions or groups of the society are at liberty to further, without endangering the stability or integrity of the society, without destroying the *virtù* of the republic. Which, according to Machiavelli happens, if these groups either have no interest in the political activities ("the business of government"), or are able to promote their own interests in legislative matters of the society uninhibited.

Let me out the question in upside down, what are those issues that this sense *could not be tolerated*, because they destroy *virtù*, the civic virtue and thus disrupt society? To start with, we need to limit down the area where the concept of toleration has the proper place and use. We need a workable analysis of the concept[24], not just a benign everyday idea of coping with the mildly irritating customs of others.

There are two instances where toleration is not the proper response to behaviour: firstly, there are those instances (things, action, practices) which should not be tolerated, because they should not be permitted at all. Such, I believe, are the likes of pedophiliacs or groups committed to violent methods. Secondly, there are those instances (things, action, practices) which should not be objected to, and which therefore do not belong to the area of toleration at all (e. g. they are not the appropriate objects of toleration). This difference is easy to see when comparing religious and racial toleration. The first, (religion) is thought[25] as the proper object of toleration, while the second (race) is not. Racial differences should not be a question of toleration, because evaluating people, labelling them, or treating them differently on the basis of their ethnic origin is not a legitimate. There is no question of tolerance, when a factory owner pays somebody less than others because of her skin colour. It is thought to be just plain wrong.

There are then two central elements in tolerance: *the first is that behaviour* (things, action, practices) *is found or thought to be objectionable*; and *the second is that one does not interfere or stop this objectionable behaviour* (things, action, practices).

There are the two central issues involved in "tolerance." Firstly, what is it that makes some behaviour objectionable in society, and secondly, when is society entitled to interfere with it? In the republican as well as liberal society, the first part of the definition is answered by defining behaviour (things, etc.) as objectionable solely from the point of view of the individual citizens. What is at stake with both theories is the protection of individuals. Yet the mere objectionable character of behaviour (things, etc.) is not a sufficient ground for public interference, and this is what the second part of the definition implies.

To clarify this issue, we need to go back to the concept of liberty, one more time. Even though Machiavelli talks a lot about freedom and liberty, this is not a liberal conception of freedom. As is well known, Machiavelli was interested in the "the liberty of the ancients" rather than "the liberty of the moderns." Concerning such a notion of liberty, Alan Ryan writes that, [w]hat counted as liberty was not license to do whatever we want, so much as it was freedom from the arbitrary, selfish, corrupt, and greedy whims of those whose power outran their self-control. The Romans, in this view, possessed individual liberty; rich men did not dare to affront the honour of the wives of their social inferiors, and nobody's property or person could be considered fair game. This was tough, tightly constrained republican freedom.[26]

But what does such a republican liberty or freedom consist of? How does it differ from the liberal freedom, and where is the place of toleration, if anywhere? What is the role of the civic virtues of republican society, and why are they so important for individual liberty?

Even many liberals think today that a liberal community cannot be sustained on the basis of legal institutions and safeguards alone, but requires certain civic virtues as well; such as tolerance, honesty, and promise-keeping. But these virtues are often considered to be "thin," as sorts of minimal commitments to issues such as fair procedures, or alertness to protect one's own interests, whereas republican virtues seem to be more substantial, more communally directed, and thus more demanding.

But in what sense? As became clear from the account above, for Machiavelli there are no universal human ends, that would require advancement as common goods in similar manner in every human society. We must also keep in mind that Machiavelli was more than a theoretical thinker an empiricist, who observed the world around him and interpreted it on the basis of his thorough knowledge of history. This is why Machiavelli does not condemn Christian virtues on moral grounds, he just says that they do not fit into the kind of world we live in, if we want a stable and an efficient society. Therefore the common goods of each society are particular; that is, variable according to prevailing circumstances. And as such, they are matters of political deliberation, competition but also surveillance.

It is also important to distinguish *republican common goods* from *communitarian common goods*, as Honohan does:

Republican politics is concerned with enabling interdependent citizens to deliberate on, and realise, the common goods of an historically evolving political community, at least as much as promoting individual interests or protecting individual rights. Emphasising responsibility for common goods sets republicanism apart from libertarian theories centred on individual rights. Emphasising that these common goods are politically realised sets republicanism apart from neutralist liberal theories which exclude substantive questions of values and the good life from politics. Finally, emphasising the political construction of the political community distinguishes republicans from those communitarians who see politics as expressing the pre-political shared values of a community.[27]

Summarising from this quote, in a republican, historically evolving and politically constructed community, its citizens are seen as interdependent and as such have the responsibility to deliberate on and realise certain substantial common goods. These responsibilities are just as important as their responsibility to protect individual rights; or their liberty to promote individual interests. But the key difference is that for the republicans, common goods are politically realised goods, while for the communitarians they are the pre-political shared values of a community.

Consequently, the republican civic virtue is more narrow than the communitarian virtue: it says nothing about family goals, marital obligations, religious beliefs, or similar shared communitarian values. Republican citizenry may establish social practices that require other virtues, but that is a different matter altogether.[28] They are not inborn or an inseparable part of the identity in the sense the communitarian "ties that bind" are.

Since republicanism has no such pre-political shared values, they come into being through the political process, from participating together with the other factions of the society. The crucial ingredient of civic virtue is the willingness to deliberate; to reflect on opinions and communicate with others. For the republicans, politics is not primarily a means for realising private interests, but a process of communication, through which common interests may be defined and realised.[29] As a result, these republican common goods cannot be defined before the political procedure – as the communitarians do. This is the lifeblood of the republican society: various, and often opposing interests competing and watching over each other in the political fields, thus furthering their own goals, learning new things, preserving individual liberty and creating common goods, all within the political sphere, meaning here mainly the framework of law. But surely this ideal – the rule of law – is something that the liberal theory also dearly endorses. So where is the crucial difference between these two theories?

## Tolerance, What Tolerance?

It is finally here that we can return to the question of tolerance. Summarising my analysis so far, as a starting-point, tolerance discussed here concerns public institutions. Further, it means that some or other kind of behaviour is found objectionable. This is, of course, often the case in most or all spheres of human life, yet the central question of tolerance is, should we do something about the offending behaviour? Thus this latter question can be rephrased in institutional context as whether such behaviour is to be interfered with or banned. So instead of trying to settle what the common goods of a republican society are,[30] let us try outline, what sort of behaviour (things, etc.) should be banned in a republican society. I tried to show in the last chapter, that political activities, furtherance of private goals, surveillance of the activities of others is in no way objectionable to the republicans – nor to liberals. Quite the contrary, and this is summoned in the Machiavellian "pluralism," which ran contrary to a lot of earlier republicanism: the way to civic glory is not in the united mind and the prohibition of discords in the society, because it is just these discords that prevent prevailing of private interests and thus are the first ladder to liberty. In this sense the republicans endorsing this view are surely tolerant.

Yet Honohan claims that republican communication and deliberation,

> [i]nvolves more than tolerance. Citizens listen to other points of view, are prepared to explain their own position and to revise it in deliberation. But it does not presuppose consensus; there will be strong differences on how to interpret, prioritise and realise common goods. Learning to deal with conflict is itself an important part of civic virtue. Citizens need to be able to exercise independent judgement, but accept decisions when made in a fair public procedure. But they are vigilant with respect to abuses of power, public or private. They are prepared to raise and support others who raise

issues of concern in the public arena, and to defend the interests of fellow citizens subject to injustices as well as defending themselves. This may involve opposing laws which undermine freedom, including civil disobedience and direct action...[31]

The phrase interesting here is that the republican virtues in fact "involve more than tolerance." I am not sure what that exactly means, but I suppose it denotes that there is some kind of behaviour (things, etc.), which can – or maybe even should – be prohibited in a republican society, that is somehow destroys the attempts to create a flourishing republican society. In other words, these are the necessary requirements, something of which deviation is not allowed in the sense meant by "toleration." I suppose this is accounts to the same thing as Steven Kautz, who argues from the liberal standing-point that the republicans "worry that the indiscriminate practice of tolerance weakens the civic and moral virtues that are necessary for self-government."[32] This means that in a republican society there are, however, certain common goods, which are vital for individual liberty. But what are they?

Recall that Machiavelli claimed that civic glory fails to be attained, if the various groups in society either have no interest in the political activities, or are able to promote their own interests in legislative matters of the society uninhibited. This latter possibility is ruled out by the rule of law, which constraints the way private interests are promoted. Thus the common goods emerging are results of this process, and only the become *legitimate* common goods. Since there are no pre-political common goods, as the communitarian goods are, there are no standards which would ban or prohibit some private goals as *objectionable before the process*. The promotion of private interests, whatever they may be – seen as offensive, disgusting or unfair individually or within some groups – is then not, where we are to look for those common goods, which could legitimately be interfered with or prohibited, that is, not tolerated. As in liberal theory, the political process (negotiating, bargaining, deliberation) )operating under the rule of law is supposed to take care of that.

What we are left with, is then the first possibility given by Machiavelli, that is, that the various groups in society have no interest in the political activities. If groups themselves opt out of the business of politics, retreat to their own customs and manners, pay no attention to what is happening in the society around them, do not bring out in public their goals, do not deliberate on nor participate on the formation of the goals of society, this will have fatal effects firstly on liberty, and then on civic virtues and flourishing of the society. Such isolation and detachment from the political life – whatever the reasons are, stagnant identity, feeling of isolation, frustration, feeling of being treated unfairly, religious or ideological aspirations – is, and always has been the greatest fear of the republican theory. These, I claim, form the kind of public goods or bads, that the republican society can not tolerate. Such behaviour is objectionable and should be interfered with.

In this sense then, republicans surely are intolerant. As Kautz says,

> [r]epublicans are intolerant. It goes almost without saying that republican political communities depend on the virtu of patriotic citizens to a higher degree that do other forms of government... But since virtue and patriotism do not emerge naturally or spontaneously, partisans of republican politics have always argued that a more or less "repressive" moral and civic education, including cencorship among other species of intolerance, would be required in order to bring into being a virtuous republican citizenry.[33]

My suggestion is that they are, it is the positive tasks of civic education, the deviance of which is not tolerated in republican societies; and these tasks are surprisingly many, as described by Steven Levine:

As with Liberalism, the basis of Republican views on institutional and state design is grounded upon its prior anthropology. Institutions should be shaped with the goal of making possible the highest level of self-determination by a citizenry. This ideal has large ramification... In the political sphere, this would mean attempting to foster: 1) a robust public sphere in which debate and dialogue can flourish, and 2) a robust civil society in which agents can exercise their capacities in sub-political institutions which at certain times circulate into the political. To foster both of these things would obviously require radical institutional change. First, the public sphere would have to be protected from becoming oligarchic and subject to the disproportionate influence of a single faction. In a modern context this would require both "negative" and "positive" changes. Negatively, the existing media system would have to be radically decentralized. But this decentralization does not mean that we would need to get government out of the picture leaving the de-centralization in the hands of capital. Quite the contrary. Decentralization would also mean taking capital out of the media system as much as possible. To make this happen would require not just regulation, but the positive enactment of new centers of communication and connectivity. To really effect this requires the rethinking of such things as urban planning, transportation, environmental policy, etc.[34]

It is then here that liberalism and republicanism part company most dramatically. Liberalism does not require its citizens to participate and deliberate; they are at liberty to do that, if they wish, but in no way can they be forced to do. Republicanism evidently is justified to go rather far in the provision of this public good.

### A Few Final Words

It is now time to the the last look at pluralism and tolerance. Concerning tolerance, Machiavelli would probably not see it as a concept of particular worth, and certainly not as universally obligating. He would treat it just as he would any other concept of moral connotation, that is, whether it are instrumentally useful for the attainment of civic glory. This is, I suppose a lame and certainly not a surprising conclusion, yet I think it does have an important connection to the current debate of social philosophy, that between liberalism and its various critics, as I have tried to show here.

What we have found here is firstly that, Lockean tolerance was only limited tolerance in the sense that it accommodated only visions which already shared a common understanding of a certain common good, that was, the existence of a Christian god. For the very same reason it was never pluralistic in that it didn't truly accommodate nor acknowledge different and incommensurable visions of good. Republicanism, on the other hand, is pluralist, at least in the reading originating from Machiavelli, and at least in the sense that it acknowledges the existence of a multitude of moral codes and human ends. This, of course, was something, which is today often called *descriptive pluralism* in opposition to *prescriptive* or *ethical pluralism*, which states that there exists a plurality of moral codes and human ends, which *cannot be reduced to one basic form*. I do not know, whether Machiavelli was a pluralist also in this prescriptive sense, at least Berlin seems to think so. Machiavelli was, after all, an empiricist, and was therefore more interested in dealing with the fact of plurality in political life, than figuring out, whether there was some metaphysical truth involved.

But surely there is something very wrong in the whole conversation here. This cannot be the kind of concept of tolerance that it is imagined to be, hoped to be, what we really mean be it, what its prescriptive content is supposed to be? And since the liberal conception of tolerance presented here is a historical, it may just as well be wrong? Is it not the case that in the heart of the concept is a universal ideal of tolerance towards all human beings, not just the ones we already agree with on something fundamental? At minimum, I suggest, it contains the kind of the wait-and-see-moment, before passing a judgement on the other party's behaviour (things, etc.). But let us then continue the discussion from the idea that tolerance does indeed mean that there are things we do not like, and yet we do not interfere with them, and work further on that basis for a workable and an analytical, universal definition.

## NOTES

1. Berlin, Isaiah: "A Special Supplement: The Question of Machiavelli," *The New York Review of Books*, Volume 17, Number 7, November 4, 1971.
2. As was summarised by Professor Timo Airaksinen during the discussions of the seminar.
3. No wonder then that "The Art of War" was one of his publications; see Dacres, Translated by Peter Whitehorne and Edward, (ed.) *Machiavelli, Volume I: The Art of War; and The Prince*. The Project Gutenberg Ebook. 2005.
4. This is another intriguing aspect of Machiavelli's thinking, which came out well during the sessions of the seminar.

5. I am, of course, not trying to cover the varieties of republican theories here; I just concentrate on the kind of thinking that would seem to me to be plausibly and consistently arising out of Machiavelli's thinking.
6. Honohan, Iseult. *Civic Republicanism*. London: Routledge, 2002.
7. According to the *New Oxford American Dictionary* (2nd edition), the etymological foundations of the term come from the 16th century, late Middle English, denoting the action of bearing hardship, or the ability to bear pain and hardship. This term, on the other hand, was received via Old French from Latin *tolerantia*, from *tolerare*.
8. Grey, John. "Pluralism and Toleration in Contemporary Political Philosophy." *Political Studies* Vol. 48 Issue 2 (2000): p. 323.
9. Paine, Robert, "Aboriginality, authenticity, and the Settler word," p. 106 in A. P. Cohen (ed.) *Signifying Identities – Anthropological Perspectives on Boundaries and Contested Values*,
10. Grey 2000: p. 323.
11. Berlin, Isaiah, and Oxford University of. *Two Concepts of Liberty: An Inaugural Lecture Delivered Before the University of Oxford on 31 October, 1958. Inaugural Lecture*. Oxford: Clarendon Press, 1958.
12. Skinner, Quentin. *Machiavelli: A Very Short Introduction*, Oxford; New York: Oxford University Press, 2000.
13. Ibid. 52.
14. Ibid.
15. Ibid. 54.
16. Machiavelli's point here is that states do not come into being naturally, but need somebody (a founder or a law-giver) to establish their basic institutions. This is because without a political structure there is no basis for people on which to form an agreement to live together; which, of course is an interesting idea, especially in relation to the social contract theory, which will only appear somewhat later, especially in Thomas Hobbes' works.
17. Skinner 2000, p. 61
18. This line of argument is not of interest here, however interesting it as such is. So I will not deal with it any further.
19. Berlin, Isaiah, and Ramin Jahanbegloo. *Conversations With Isaiah Berlin*. London: Peter Halban Publishers, 1992, p. 54.
20. Ibid. 56.
21. Ibid. 66.
22. See also for instance Buttle, Nicholas. "Republican Constitutionalism: A Roman Ideal." *The Journal of Political Philosophy*, Volume 9, Number 3 (2001): 331–49.
23. Skinner 2000, p.66.
24. I am grateful for Professor Heta Gylling for useful advice and discussion concerning the analysis of the concept of tolerance.
25. There are, no doubt, echoes of Lockean tolerance to be found here.
26. Ryan, Alan. "Isaiah Berlin: Political Theory and Liberal Culture." *Annu. Rev. Polit. Sci.* 2:345–62 (1999), p. 354.
27. Honohan 2002, p. 1
28. Ibid. 164.
29. Ibid. 161.

30. Since the question here is of particular and changing substantial goods, it would probably not even be possible to determine them at this general and abstract level.
31. Ibid. 162.
32. Kautz, Steven J. "Liberalism and the Idea of Toleration." *American Journal of Political Science* Vol. 37, No. 2 (1993), p. 610.
33. Ibid. 614.
34. Levine, Steven M. "A Republican Left." *OTR Politics*, January, 2004, Electronic source: http://www.fluxfactory.org/otr/levinerepublican.htm (accessed 29.9.2006).

# CONTRIBUTORS

Timo Airaksinen – Professor of Philosophy at the University of Helsinki, Finland.

Hubert Schleichert – Professor Emeritus of Philosophy at the University of Konstanz, Germany.

Manfred J. Holler – Professor of Economics in the Institute of Socioeconomics at the University of Hamburg, Germany.

Leonidas Donskis – Member of the European Parliament (2009–2014); Visiting Professor of Social and Political Theory at Vytautas Magnus University in Kaunas, Lithuania.

Cătălin Avramescu – Reader in the Department of Political Science at the University of Bucharest, Romania.

Juhana Lemetti – D.Soc.Sci., Researcher in the Department of Economic and Political Studies at the University of Helsinki, Finland.

Olli Loukola – Docent of Philosophy at the University of Helsinki, Finland.

# INDEX

### A

Agathocles, 8;
Alexander VI, Pope, 29, 30, 34, 42, 52, 55, 56, 61

### B

Bacon, Sir Francis, 58, 65
Bandello, Matteo, 58
Bentivogli, (Messer) Giovanni, 43
Borgia, Cesare, 27–30, 33-34; 38, 42–44, 46, 52, 55
Bulgakov, Mikhail, 52
Bull, George, 5–7,
Burnham, James, 54

### C

Caesar, Gaius Julius, 21, 31, 40
Carnedes, 45
Cato, 45
Claudius, Appius, 40–41
Clement VII, Pope, 42, 50
Confucius, 15, 17
Copleston, Frederick, 62–63
Crick, B., 8–9

### D

Diogenes, 45
Dylan, Bob, 27

### E

Erasmus of Rotterdam, Pius Desiderius, 53, 55

## F

Fabritius, Carel, 50
Fichte, Johann Gottlieb, 54
Frederic II (Frederic the Great), 17–18, 23

## G

Gauss, Christian, 31
Gelder, Aert de, 50
Grazia, Sebastian de, 7
Guicciardini, Francesco, 28, 46, 68

## H

Hegel, Georg Wilhelm Friedrich, 15, 21, 54
Herder, Johann Gottlieb von, 54
Henry VII, 64
Henry VIII, 50
Hitler, Adolf, 21, 54
Hobbes, Thomas, 22–23, 35–36, 70, 76, 79–89, 100, 107

## J

Joly, Maurice, 61–62
Julius II, Pope, 10, 29, 43, 59

## K

Katherine of Aragon, 50
Koestler, Arthur, 54

## L

Lun Yu, 15, 17
Luther, Martin, 15, 25, 50, 55

## M

Machiavelli, Niccolò, 3–47, 49, 51–77, 79–81, 83–89, 91–93, 95–107
Mansfield, Harvey C., 62, 65, 76
Marius, 31, 40
Marlowe, Christopher, 53,
Marx, Karl, 54, 56
Medici, Giuliano, 42, 68
Medici, Giulio de' (Pope Clement VII), 42, 50–51,
Medici, Giovanni de' (Pope Leo X), 28, 50–51, 68
Medici, Lorenzo de' (Lorenzo Magnifico), 28, 42, 46, 56, 59, 68
Medici, Piero di, 28
Medicis, the, 18, 28, 30, 44, 50, 52, 56, 61, 65, 68
Mo Di, 19–20
Molière, 57
Molina, Tirso de, 57
Montesquieu, Charles Louis de Secondat, Baron de la, Brede et de, 61–62
More, Sir Thomas, 53, 55

## N

Napoleon Bonaparte, 21, 54, 59, 75
Napoleon III, 54, 62
Nietzsche, Friedrich, 56

## O

Orco, (Messer) Remirro de, 33–34, 36, 46
Orwell, George, 54

## P

Peter, Saint, 42, 53
Petrucci, Alfonso, Cardinal, 50
Plutarch, 56
Porto, Luigi da, 58
Prezzolini, Giuseppe, 7

R

Rabelais, François, 55
Raphael (Raffaello Sanzio), 50
Rembrandt (Rembrandt Harmensz van Rijn), 49–50
Romulus, 29–30, 38–39, 43
Rossi, Luigi de', Cardinal, 50–51


S

Savonarola, Girolamo, 56, 61, 67, 70, 72, 74
Scharfstein, Ben-Ami, 21
Shakespeare, William, 37, 51, 53, 58, 60
Sixtus IV, Pope, 42
Skinner, Quentin, 5–7, 47, 82–84, 86, 88–89, 91, 96–97, 100
Soderini, Piero, 31, 56
Spinoza, Benedict (Baruch), 18,
Stalin, Joseph, 21, 54
Stendhal, 57–60
Sylla, 31,


V

Van Eyck, Jan, 49,
Voltaire, 20, 57, 70


W

Weber, Max, 27–28, 34, 36, 42, 45–47
Worden, Blair, 64, 66

# VIBS

The **Value Inquiry Book Series** is co-sponsored by:

Adler School of Professional Psychology
American Indian Philosophy Association
American Maritain Association
American Society for Value Inquiry
Association for Process Philosophy of Education
Canadian Society for Philosophical Practice
Center for Bioethics, University of Turku
Center for Professional and Applied Ethics, University of North Carolina at Charlotte
Central European Pragmatist Forum
Centre for Applied Ethics, Hong Kong Baptist University
Centre for Cultural Research, Aarhus University
Centre for Professional Ethics, University of Central Lancashire
Centre for the Study of Philosophy and Religion, University College of Cape Breton
Centro de Estudos em Filosofia Americana, Brazil
College of Education and Allied Professions, Bowling Green State University
College of Liberal Arts, Rochester Institute of Technology
Concerned Philosophers for Peace
Conference of Philosophical Societies
Department of Moral and Social Philosophy, University of Helsinki
Gannon University
Gilson Society
Haitian Studies Association
Ikeda University
Institute of Philosophy of the High Council of Scientific Research, Spain
International Academy of Philosophy of the Principality of Liechtenstein
International Association of Bioethics
International Center for the Arts, Humanities, and Value Inquiry
International Society for Universal Dialogue
Natural Law Society
Philosophical Society of Finland
Philosophy Born of Struggle Association
Philosophy Seminar, University of Mainz
Pragmatism Archive at The Oklahoma State University
R.S. Hartman Institute for Formal and Applied Axiology
Research Institute, Lakeridge Health Corporation
Russian Philosophical Society
Society for Existential Analysis
Society for Iberian and Latin-American Thought
Society for the Philosophic Study of Genocide and the Holocaust
Unit for Research in Cognitive Neuroscience, Autonomous University of Barcelona
Whitehead Research Project
Yves R. Simon Institute

Titles Published

Volumes 1 - 192 see www.rodopi.nl

193. Brendan Sweetman, *The Vision of Gabriel Marcel: Epistemology, Human Person, the Transcendent.* A volume in **Philosophy and Religion**

194. Danielle Poe and Eddy Souffrant, Editors, *Parceling the Globe: Philosophical Explorations in Globalization, Global Behavior, and Peace.* A volume in **Philosophy of Peace**

195. Josef Šmajs, *Evolutionary Ontology: Reclaiming the Value of Nature by Transforming Culture.* A volume in **Central-European Value Studies**

196. Giuseppe Vicari, *Beyond Conceptual Dualism: Ontology of Consciousness, Mental Causation, and Holism in John R. Searle's Philosophy of Mind.* A volume in **Cognitive Science**

197. Avi Sagi, *Tradition vs. Traditionalism: Contemporary Perspectives in Jewish Thought.* Translated from Hebrew by Batya Stein. A volume in **Philosophy and Religion**

198. Randall E. Osborne and Paul Kriese, Editors, *Global Community: Global Security.* A volume in **Studies in Jurisprudence**

199. Craig Clifford, *Learned Ignorance in the Medicine Bow Mountains: A Reflection on Intellectual Prejudice.* A volume in **Lived Values: Valued Lives**

200. Mark Letteri, *Heidegger and the Question of Psychology: Zollikon and Beyond.* A volume in **Philosophy and Psychology**

201. Carmen R. Lugo-Lugo and Mary K. Bloodsworth-Lugo, Editors, *A New Kind of Containment: "The War on Terror," Race, and Sexuality.* A volume in **Philosophy of Peace**

202. Amihud Gilead, *Necessity and Truthful Fictions: Panenmentalist Observations.* A volume in **Philosophy and Psychology**

203. Fernand Vial, *The Unconscious in Philosophy, and French and European Literature: Nineteenth and Early Twentieth Century.* A volume in **Philosophy and Psychology**

204. Adam C. Scarfe, Editor, *The Adventure of Education: Process Philosophers on Learning, Teaching, and Research*. A volume in **Philosophy of Education**

205. King-Tak Ip, Editor, *Environmental Ethics: Intercultural Perspectives*. A volume in **Studies in Applied Ethics**

206. Evgenia Cherkasova, *Dostoevsky and Kant: Dialogues on Ethics*. A volume in **Social Philosophy**

207. Alexander Kremer and John Ryder, Editors, *Self and Society: Central European Pragmatist Forum*, Volume Four. A volume in **Central European Value Studies**

208. Terence O'Connell, *Dialogue on Grief and Consolation*. A volume in **Lived Values, Valued Lives**

209. Craig Hanson, *Thinking about Addiction: Hyperbolic Discounting and Responsible Agency*. A volume in **Social Philosophy**

210. Gary G. Gallopin, *Beyond Perestroika: Axiology and the New Russian Entrepreneurs*. A volume in **Hartman Institute Axiology Studies**

211. Tuija Takala, Peter Herissone-Kelly, and Søren Holm, Editors, *Cutting Through the Surface: Philosophical Approaches to Bioethics*. A volume in **Values in Bioethics**

212. Neena Schwartz: *A Lab of My Own*. A volume in **Lived Values, Valued Lives**

213. Krzysztof Piotr Skowroński, *Values and Powers: Re-reading the Philosophical Tradition of American Pragmatism*. A volume in **Central European Value Studies**

214. Matti Häyry, Tuija Takala, Peter Herissone-Kelly and Gardar Árnason, Editors, *Arguments and Analysis in Bioethics*. A volume in **Values in Bioethics**

215. Anders Nordgren, *For Our Children: The Ethics of Animal Experimentation in the Age of Genetic Engineering*. A volume in **Values in Bioethics**

216. James R. Watson, Editor, *Metacide: In the Pursuit of Excellence*. A volume in **Holocaust and Genocide Studies**

217. Andrew Fitz-Gibbon, Editor, *Positive Peace: Reflections on Peace Education, Nonviolence, and Social Change*. A volume in **Philosophy of Peace**

218. Christopher Berry Gray, *The Methodology of Maurice Hauriou: Legal, Sociological, Philosophical*. A volume in **Studies in Jurisprudence**

219. Mary K. Bloodsworth-Lugo and Carmen R. Lugo-Lugo, *Containing (Un)American Bodies: Race, Sexuality, and Post-9/11 Constructions of Citizenship*. A volume in **Philosophy of Peace**

220. Roland Faber, Brian G. Henning, Clinton Combs, Editors, *Beyond Metaphysics? Explorations in Alfred North Whitehead's Late Thought*. A volume in **Contemporary Whitehead Studies**

221. John G. McGraw, *Intimacy and Isolation (Intimacy and Aloneness: A Multi-Volume Study in Philosophical Psychology, Volume One)*, A volume in **Philosophy and Psychology**

222. Janice L. Schultz-Aldrich, Introduction and Edition, *"Truth" is a Divine Name, Hitherto Unpublished Papers of Edward A. Synan, 1918-1997*. A volume in **Gilson Studies**

223. Larry A. Hickman, Matthew Caleb Flamm, Krzysztof Piotr Skowroński and Jennifer A. Rea, Editors, *The Continuing Relevance of John Dewey: Reflections on Aesthetics, Morality, Science, and Society*. A volume in **Central European Value Studies**

224. Hugh P. McDonald, *Creative Actualization: A Meliorist Theory of Values*. A volume in **Studies in Pragmatism and Values**

225. Rob Gildert and Dennis Rothermel, Editors, *Remembrance and Reconciliation*. A volume in **Philosophy of Peace**

226. Leonidas Donskis, Editor, *Niccolò Machiavelli: History, Power, and Virtue*. A volume in **Philosophy, Literature, and Politics**

www.ingramcontent.com/pod-product-compliance
Lightning Source LLC
Chambersburg PA
CBHW030117010526
44116CB00005B/285